## DATE DUE

|  |  |  |  |
|---|---|---|---|
|  |  |  |  |
|  |  |  |  |
|  |  |  |  |
|  |  |  |  |
|  |  |  |  |
|  |  |  |  |
|  |  |  |  |
|  |  |  |  |
|  |  |  |  |
|  |  |  |  |
|  |  |  |  |
|  |  |  |  |
|  |  |  |  |
|  |  |  |  |
|  |  |  |  |
|  |  |  |  |
|  |  |  |  |
|  |  |  |  |
|  |  |  | PRINTED IN U.S.A. |

# ALSACE

*gastronomique*

LA TABLE ALSACIENNE

# ALSACE
## *gastronomique*

## SUE STYLE

FOREWORD BY ANNE WILLAN

PHOTOGRAPHY BY MARIANNE MAJERUS

SERIES EDITOR: MARIE-PIERRE MOINE

**ABBEVILLE PRESS PUBLISHERS**
NEW YORK  LONDON  PARIS

First published in the United States of America in
1996 by Abbeville Press
488 Madison Avenue
New York, NY 10022

First published in Great Britain in 1996 by
Conran Octopus Limited
37 Shelton Street
London WC2H 9HN

ISBN 0-7892-0235-2

Project Editors ALISON BOLUS,
CHARLOTTE COLEMAN-SMITH
Commissioning Editor SARAH PEARCE
Art Editor KAREN BOWEN
Text Editor WENDY DALLAS
Recipe Editor JACQUI HINES
Home Economist JANE SUTHERING
Production JILL BEED, SUE BAYLISS
Typesetting LIZA BRUML

Printed in Singapore

NOTE ON RECIPES Both metric and imperial
quantities are given. Use either all metric or all
imperial, as the two are not interchangeable.

# CONTENTS

# FOREWORD

A combination of French flair and German generosity, no wonder Alsatian cooking is so successful! Onion tart, *poulet au riesling*, venison stew with chanterelles, *Spätzle*, plum strudel. As I roam through the dishes in Sue Style's attractive tour of the region, so many good meals come to mind. There was that amazing *choucroute* piled high with sausages and different smoked meats that we tackled – confronted might be a better word – that rainy day near the station in Colmar. I could not believe that hunger might strike again, but the array of terrines and tarts in a nearby *traiteur* proved me wrong. Preparations for a wedding were in progress and the spread was a still life of the pastry cook's art.

Good food begins with good ingredients and Alsace can claim an abundance. The broad plain of the Rhine is lined with fruit trees, source of the famous Alsatian *alcools blancs*. Some of the rare wild boar and deer in France shelter in the rugged Vosges mountains, home also to wild mushrooms and cows who provide the notoriously redolent Munster cheese. Don't forget the breads: Germanic rye breads, brioche-like *Kougelhopfs* which come in sweet and savoury versions, and the many breakfast rolls with names like bird's nest or beehive. As for the wine, a quick stroll in any of the two dozen wine villages that nestle at the eastern foot of the mountains reveals a prosperity dating to medieval times and beyond.

The adjective picturesque could have been coined for Alsace, and photographer Marianne Majerus is in her element, bringing us vivid views of orchards and vegetable gardens, family tables and bakery windows, geranium-lined streets, and the towering multiple gables of Strasbourg, the capital. In one small province, Alsace offers so much, with fine country restaurants thicker on the ground than anywhere else in France. Don't miss its charms!

*FAR RIGHT A beautiful wrought iron
sign outside the Pharmacie du Cygne in Colmar
depicting the apothecary at work.
RIGHT Decorated eau-de-vie bottles containing
fruit spirits for which Alsace – and particularly
the Vosges region – is famous.
BELOW Dusk descends upon Kaysersberg,
whose houses and public buildings
are always exquisitely decorated for the
Christmas period.*

# INTRODUCTION

Popular tradition would have us believe that as the Sun King came over the Col de Saverne from Lorraine in 1681 to inspect his new province of Alsace, he was heard to exclaim, '*Quel beau jardin!*' The visitor to Alsace today, arriving from the north by approximately the same route, sweeps down a motorway carved through pink sandstone and passes beneath the *passerelle à gîbier* (footbridge for game), to be greeted by a sign declaring proudly, *Vous êtes en Alsace!* Below lies – still – the beautiful garden of Alsace.

Along its narrow northern edge and its western side are the densely forested Vosges mountains, home to wild boar, deer and mushrooms, domain of huntsmen, walkers and cross-country skiers. Sheltering at the feet of the Vosges are proud and prosperous vineyard villages, their colourful half-timbered houses topped with steeply slanting roofs made of the characteristic 'beaver's tail' round-ended tiles. The vine-clad foothills give way in their turn to the fertile Rhine basin, nowadays a huge granary, maize field and cabbage plantation, with a little room left for market gardeners and fishermen. And then comes the Rhine, grand and impressive, even with hundreds of kilometres still to go to its mouth near Rotterdam. To the south, the gently undulating landscape of the Sundgau, with its grazing pastures and orchards and its countless carp ponds, rises up finally into the Swiss Jura which mark the southern limit of the region.

Alsace is the old geographical name used to designate a province which nowadays comprises two *départements*: the Haut-Rhin and the Bas-Rhin. To most of us for whom north is 'up' and south is 'down', it is confusing to find that the upper – northern – part of Alsace corresponds to the Bas-Rhin, the lower Rhine (whose capital is Strasbourg), while the southern *département* is the Haut-Rhin or upper Rhine (headed by Colmar). The majestic river flows steadily on, however, oblivious to the points of the compass and to preconceived notions of what is 'up' and what is 'down'.

In the three hundred and fifty years since the Sun King first gathered Alsace under the wing of France, the border with Germany has been pushed from the Rhine up into the Vosges (1871), back to the Rhine (1918), up into the Vosges again (1939) and has finally settled down once more on the Rhine (1945). Languages and dialects have waxed and waned, depending on whether the government of the day was based in Paris or Berlin; towns and villages have been destroyed, rebuilt, devastated and reconstructed once more. The end result of this tumultuous history is the Alsace of today.

By virtue of its geography, even in peace time the region has always been a *lieu de passage*, a sort of corridor, and therefore open to change and new ideas. Yet throughout its embattled history – perhaps precisely because of it – Alsace has clung fiercely to its traditions, and above all to its great gastronomic heritage. The result – a firmly established cultural base which has nonetheless been modified by outside influences – makes Alsace an unusually interesting gastronomic crossroads at which to meet.

As in other regions of France it was the Romans who established the foundations of the great cuisine and the fine wines of Alsace today. Apart from vines, they also introduced fruit, vegetables and herbs hitherto unknown this far north. But for them, Alsace might never have had cherries and thus no Kirsch; no cabbages, therefore no *choucroute*; no asparagus, the focus of many a joyous springtime pilgrimage. Foie gras was another Roman introduction, as was a certain sort of soft, *gnocchi*-like pasta. (To this day the *alsaciens* make extensive use of all kinds of pasta.)

The Benedictines must take the credit for further developing the gastronomy of Alsace and giving it much of its present-day importance and character. They put their considerable talents to work on wine (for the communion table), *eaux-de-vie* (for medicinal purposes), beer (to quench the thirst), cheese (they were past masters in the art of making Munster, see page 78) and pork salting and smoking. The Benedictine Abbot Buchinger's famous *Kochbuch*, published in 1671 and directed at both religious communities and lay people, provides a fascinating chronicle of seventeenth-century diet and mores. Some of the abbot's recipes – for pâtés, terrines, noodles and herb marinades for spit-roasted meat – sound reassuringly familiar. Others, such as the one for beavers' tails or a lavishly spiced sweet-sour dish of boiled beef, might appeal less to contemporary tastes.

The region is famous above all for its wine, cheese, *charcuterie* – and bread. While in much of France bread boils down to *baguettes* in their various manifestations, Alsace has more to offer. Flours made from wholewheat, rye and spelt (a primitive species of wheat) are mixed with white flour to give a seemingly endless range of well-flavoured textured loaves, some sprinkled with poppy seeds, others with sunflower or sesame seeds. *Kougelhopf*, a light, brioche-type, turban-shaped bread, comes in sweet and savoury versions, the latter speckled with bacon and crowned with walnuts instead of almonds.

The forests and mountains of the region have always been rich in game. Today, one of the delights of autumn is the range of game dishes to be found at the best tables, accompanied by the regulation *Spätzle* (see recipe page 41). Fish is another favourite: as long ago as 1580 Montaigne commented, while on his travels in Alsace, on the exquisite way in which it was prepared by local cooks. From the Vosges to the Sundgau the rivers, streams and ponds are well furnished with trout and carp; today crayfish, eels, sander and even salmon are once more fished from the Rhine.

Perhaps the greatest ambassadors for Alsace are its wines. The distinctive, slim, elegant bottle (known as a *flûte*) is labelled – unusually for France – after the *cépage*, or type of grape from which the wine is made: Riesling, Gewurztraminer, Pinot Gris (also known as Tokay-Pinot Gris), Muscat, Pinot Blanc, Sylvaner or Pinot Noir. Depending on the grape variety and on the maker, the wines can be austere or accessible, full-bodied or lean,

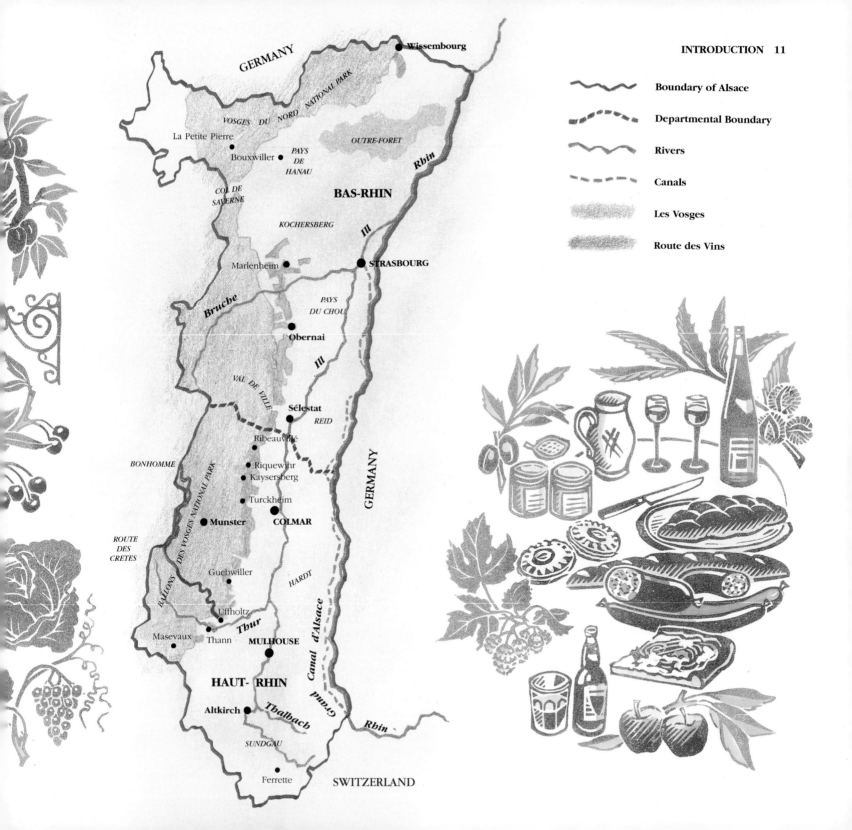

GERMANY

Wissembourg

*VOSGES DU NORD NATIONAL PARK*

La Petite Pierre

*OUTRE-FORET*

Bouxwiller

*PAYS DE HANAU*

*Rhin*

*COL DE SAVERNE*

**BAS-RHIN**

*KOCHERSBERG*

*Ill*

Marlenheim

STRASBOURG

*Bruche*

*PAYS DU CHOU*

**Obernai**

*Ill*

*VAL DE VILLE*

**Sélestat**

*RIED*

*BONHOMME*

Ribeauvillé

Riquewihr

Kaysersberg

GERMANY

Turckheim

**Munster**

**COLMAR**

*DES VOSGES NATIONAL PARK*

*ROUTE DES CRETES*

Guebwiller

*HARDT*

*BALLONS*

Uffholtz

*Thur*

Masevaux

Thann

**MULHOUSE**

*Canal d'Alsace*

**HAUT- RHIN**

Altkirch

*Thalbach*

*Grand*

*Rhin*

*SUNDGAU*

Ferrette

SWITZERLAND

Boundary of Alsace

Departmental Boundary

Rivers

Canals

Les Vosges

Route des Vins

intensely aromatic or light and neutral. Contrary to popular belief, the wines of Alsace are almost always dry. In a category of their own are the naturally sweet late-harvest (*vendanges tardives*) and botrytis-affected (*sélection de grains nobles*) wines (see page 59).

Perhaps because of its proximity to both Germany and Switzerland, Alsace is somewhat more advanced in matters ecological than other parts of France. (The leader of France's Green Party, Antoine Waechter, is an *alsacien*.) There are increasing numbers of organic wine growers, butchers whose meat comes from animals raised without the use of hormones and allowed to graze and frolic freely in the fields, cheese-makers who specialize in *fromages biologiques* and markets selling organic and biodynamic produce.

Springtime is a fine time to be in Alsace. The roads are traffic free and in the vineyards the buds are just beginning to break on the neatly pruned vines; at their feet grow wild chives and lamb's lettuce. The wine growers are all too happy to have you taste the latest vintage. Chefs are filing away their winter menus and welcoming back the astringent notes of asparagus, rhubarb and sorrel after the robust, calorific *choucroutes* and *Baeckeoffes* of the winter months.

In the sometimes stifling heat of high summer the better known towns and vineyard villages are best avoided. This is the time to adjourn – as do the locals – to the coolness of the Vosges, to hike purposefully or wander idly, to pick bilberries, wild raspberries and blackberries, and to take in great gulps of fresh air and robust *ferme-auberge* food. The lesser known northern and southern ends of Alsace are also delightfully deserted in summer, their various hotels and *gîtes* ready to welcome visitors.

In the autumn the colours in the vineyards above the villages echo the ochres and reddish browns of the houses and rooftops. Tractors and trailers ply backwards and forwards with their precious loads of grapes for the new harvest's wine, and in the fields shiny round cabbages are cut for *choucroute nouvelle*. There's a sweetly decaying smell in the air of fermenting must, old oak vats and gently rotting cabbages. (This is not a time for wine tasting. The wine grower is more concerned and occupied with your future drinking interests than with current consumption.)

Perhaps the most beautiful time to visit Alsace is around Christmas. Then skiers take to the gentle slopes of the Vosges for a spot of cross-country or downhill ski-ing, while in the valleys the beautifully decorated and illuminated villages remind one of a child's Advent calendar. Seasonal markets are in full swing, Christmas cake and biscuit baking reaches a crescendo, festive foie gras are put up ready for the holiday. Another year draws to a close.

To many people, the 'beautiful garden of Alsace' remains – mercifully – undiscovered and under exploited. Packed into this tiny ribbon of land hardly more than 150 kilometres long and barely 30 kilometres wide are mountains, vineyards, cities and broad open spaces. With its semi-continental climate, its impressive array of medieval towns and villages, gothic cathedrals, world-class museums and polychrome half-timbered houses, not to mention its outstanding food and wines, it makes an irresistible holiday destination. Proudly French yet profoundly European, Germanic by cultural and linguistic tradition but above all fervently *alsacien*, Alsace remains – in the words of a recent campaign for the region's wines – the French exception.

*TOP A quiet corner of Kaysersberg.*
*ABOVE A gorgeous array of foie gras products on display in the window of a specialist shop in Strasbourg.*
*OPPOSITE TOP A colourful Christmas market.*
*OPPOSITE ABOVE The Fromagerie de Saint Nicolas sells local produce such as Munsters.*
*OPPOSITE RIGHT Beautiful carvings and paintings adorn the Maison Pfister in Colmar.*

*RIGHT The graceful old Domaine du Bouxhof just outside Mittelwihr. A part of the property has been restored as a gîte or holiday home.*
*BELOW Endless distant peaks unfold to the west, near the Col de Fouchy in the Vosges.*
*BOTTOM Cows graze peacefully in the Vosges, their milk destined to make Alsace's famous cheese (RIGHT): the Munster.*

*When Louis XIV first saw Alsace he was said to
have exclaimed 'Quel beau jardin!'
To this day the people of Alsace are great
vegetable gardeners and no self-
respecting family is without its neatly tended plot
where potatoes, carrots and cabbages
vie for space with diverse saladings,
courgettes and tomatoes.
ABOVE LEFT A farmer's wife lifts the main crop
of potatoes for storing in the cellar.
Potatoes play an important role in the cuisine of
Alsace, from firm, waxy varieties such as
Charlotte, Stella and BF15 to the more floury
sorts like Bintje and Urgenta.
ABOVE The kitchen garden is situated
conveniently close to the house, filled with
produce to see the family through the year.
LEFT A market gardening couple prepare to take
their fresh produce to market.*

*FAR RIGHT A charming, sculpted detail on an old timber-framed house.*
*RIGHT A plateful of bretzels (see page 20) and Männala (see page 26), sweet breads that are sold around 6 December.*
*BELOW Richly decorated timbered houses line the rue Mercière leading to Strasbourg's superb gothic cathedral, built of pink Vosges sandstone between the eleventh and the fourteenth centuries.*

# NORTHERN ALSACE

Some of the more interesting – and the least visited – parts of Alsace are its extremities. The visitor who sweeps down through the Vosges with his sights set on Strasbourg seldom finds time to linger in the areas to the west and north of the city, where dense and beautiful forests alternate with rich, rolling agricultural landscapes and small viticultural enclaves. This is the top corner of Alsace, a sort of mirror image of the Sundgau in the south (see page 76). Germany lies to the east and north, Lorraine to the west. Where the Sundgau looks to Mulhouse (and to Basle), northern Alsace looks to Strasbourg. It is a land of brewers, huntsmen, mushroom gatherers, market gardeners, farmers and a few wine growers.

Our gastronomic journey through Alsace starts in the heart of the Parc Régional des Vosges du Nord in La Petite Pierre, a small fortified town which in the old days stood guard over the pass linking Lorraine with Alsace. Nowadays both the main road and the *autoroute* to the south cut through the country below it, leaving the town perched quietly on its craggy outcrop of pink sandstone, surrounded by a sea of deep green forests. A popular refuge for weekend walkers and holiday-makers and an important hunting centre, it boasts a handful of cosy hotels and a museum devoted to one of Alsace's Christmas specialities, the intricately carved wooden moulds used to shape and decorate the *anise*-flavoured *Springerle* biscuits.

Most distinctive and charming of all the Christmas baked goods, these biscuits are made from a simple dough of flour, sugar and eggs and highly seasoned with aniseed. The dough is rolled out to an even thickness and then left to dry a little. The special sculpted wooden *Springerle* mould, which may feature nativity scenes, birds, roses, stars or other motifs, is pressed firmly into the dough (or the dough into the mould) to give its imprint to the biscuit. Sometimes a hole is made in the top with a knitting needle or skewer before baking, so that a ribbon can be threaded through and the biscuit hung on the Christmas tree.

Its castle, regularly and extensively restored since the ninth century, was once owned by Count Georg-Johannes von Veldenz who has (inadvertently) given his nickname to a favourite local speciality, *pot au feu à l'oie Jerry-Hans*, a goose-rich version of the classic dish. The count, a distinguished philanthropist and patron of the arts, introduced the glass-blowing industry to northern Alsace, of which some traces still remain. La Maison du Verre et du Cristal in Meisenthal is devoted to the history of glass-making in the area, while in the gloomy little valley of Saint-Louis-lès-Bitche is the Royal Glassworks of Saint Louis. Founded in 1586 and enjoying Louis XV's royal warrant from 1767, it is still operational.

BOTTOM *The window of a house in Issenhausen, one of a number of lovely old villages in the Pays de Hanau.*
BELOW *La Petite Pierre sits perched on its craggy outcrop surounded by dense green forests, where abundant wild boar and roe deer are found.*
RIGHT *Superb old houses in the town of Bouxwiller, gaily decorated for Christmas.*

## THE PAYS DE HANAU

The road from the glass-making valleys winds its way gently down through the beech forests to Ingwiller, once an important Jewish town. This is the beginning of the Pays de Hanau, former domain of the counts of Hanau-Lichtenberg. Its capital is Bouxwiller, a small town with exquisite timbered houses and a museum devoted to the customs and traditions of the area. The Pâtisserie Isenmann on the Grand'rue is a picture at Christmas with its display of biscuits, chocolate Santas and other seasonal goodies.  Bouxwiller, according to legend, is the birthplace of the *bretzel* (see page 20). At New Year Monsieur Isenmann bakes a giant version from lightly sweetened brioche dough known as a *Neijohrsbretschtall* (New Year's *bretzel*). Such a bread was customarily given by children to their godparents as a token of their good wishes for the New Year. In return for the bread, if they were lucky, they received a present or coin.

Another local delicacy, traditional for weddings and special occasions in the Pays de Hanau, is *Hanauer Quetschtorte*, a rich confection of prunes, apple purée and *Schnapps*, perfumed with cinnamon, baked in a puff pastry shell and then topped with a lattice of puff pastry. If you arrange to visit Monsieur Isenmann on a Friday you will find him busy at the

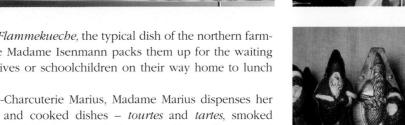

back of his shop turning out countlesss *Flammekueche,* the typical dish of the northern farming plain of Alsace (see page 21), while Madame Isenmann packs them up for the waiting queue of working mums, busy housewives or schoolchildren on their way home to lunch from the *lycée* around the corner.

On the same street, at the Boucherie-Charcuterie Marius, Madame Marius dispenses her husband's home-produced *charcuterie* and cooked dishes – *tourtes* and *tartes,* smoked *saucisses lorraines* for eating raw, and huge juicy hams on the bone – with good humoured banter, plentifully larded with topical cooking tips. From the nearby orchards and forests come apples, chestnuts and walnuts for *boudins* and *tourtes d'automne,* which combine veal and pork with fruit and nuts in a deliciously savoury manner.

South of Bouxwiller the villages of Obermodern, Buswiller and Issenhausen, with their perfectly preserved farmhouses, richly repay a visit. Especially beautiful, and distinguished by their fine timberwork and their upper galleries, are those built by the Schini family of carpenters, who came here from Switzerland in the seventeenth century in the big wave of repopulation after the Thirty Years War. These superb buildings may look like museum pieces but many are still working farms. Others, such as Monsieur Husselstein's house, a *gîte* on the main street in Buswiller, have rooms to let and serve simple regional dishes.

*ABOVE LEFT The Isenmann family in their bakery in Bouxwiller with an array of their products: (TOP) home-made confectionery, (CENTRE) Bredle (Christmas biscuits) and (BOTTOM) chocolate Santas.*

## BRETZELS

Bretzels *are a uniquely delicious speciality of Alsace. Unlike the (distantly related) dry and dusty pretzels from a packet they are tender yet chewy, with a shiny brown coat (like bagels) in which little nuggets of coarse salt are embedded. So much a part of Alsatian baking life are they that the shape is often used by bakers in the beautiful wrought-iron signs outside their shops (see page 110). The name* bretzel *is thought to be derived from the Latin word* brachium *meaning an arm: the shape of the bread suggests a pair of crossed arms attached to a solid pair of shoulders. One legend associated with the origins of this special bread involves a baker in the Pays de Hanau who was imprisoned for making rude remarks about the Count of Hanau-Lichtenberg's concubine. In order to gain his freedom, he was set the task of devising a bread through which you could see the sun three times.*

*An ingenious passer-by (an early antecedent of Superman), hearing the baker's desperate lamentations, wrenched out one of the prison bars, twisted it into the pretzel shape and passed it back to him. The delighted baker, able to see the sun through the three spaces thus created, immediately called for the count and triumphantly showed him the solution to the puzzle, thereby gaining his freedom.*

*ABOVE LEFT Hans Trapp or Rüpelz (right) searches for naughty children, while his kindly companion Christkindel (left) brings presents to good children. TOP RIGHT AND CENTRE Local farm products on sale. BOTTOM A selection of Christmas beers. OPPOSITE The Outre-Forêt.*

# OUTRE-FORET

The area north of Haguenau and its forest is familiarly known as Outre-Forêt – 'beyond the forest'. On its eastern and northern edges lie two villages famous for their pottery. The huge, decorated earthenware terrine from which a *Baeckeoffe* (see page 100) is customarily served will quite probably have been thrown in Soufflenheim, while the little blue-grey stoneware jug containing the house Edelzwicker wine (see page 49) will doubtless have been fired in a kiln in Betschdorf.

Outre-Forêt has some of the loveliest villages in all of Alsace. Their meticulously well-kept houses are roughcast in white between the dark, often intricately decorated beams. At the front are carefully tended vegetable gardens where neat rows of leeks, cabbages, celery root and lamb's lettuce are interspersed with pot marigolds, borage and the occasional hollyhock. In one corner is a barely contained patch of horseradish (see page 30).

Just short of Wissembourg lie Alsace's most northerly (and probably most ancient) vineyards. After the Second World War, wine growers from the villages of Cleebourg, Rott, Steinseltz and Oberhoffen grouped together to form the Cave Vinicole de Cleebourg. They make outstanding Pinot Auxerrois (an aromatic variant of Pinot Blanc) and Pinot Gris; particularly fine are those from named sites (*lieux-dits*) such as Brandhof and Karchweg. The clay soils and northerly climate of this tiny vineyard area give wines a certain finesse and elegance. The unusually long-necked *flûte* in which they are bottled is also elegant, if a little impractical for the wine cellar.

## FLAMMEKUECHE

*A speciality of northern Alsace,* Flammekueche *consists of paper-thin bread dough spread with cream and/or* fromage blanc, *finely sliced onions and diced bacon. Correctly prepared, it is baked on the floor of a wood-fired bread oven, licked by the dying flames (*Flamme*) of the fire – hence its ash-dusted underside and its often carbonized corners. Served on a board and cut in quarters, the sections are either folded over or rolled up and eaten with the fingers (or with knife and fork for the more fastidious or those with heat-sensitive fingers).*

Flammekueche *was a simple farmhouse dish which developed from the once-weekly baking day. When the main bread batch was finished there was often a little piece of dough left over – and a lot of residual heat in the oven. From the larder came a pot of cream or* fromage blanc, *a slab of bacon and an onion. The* alsacien *spirit of economy was combined with a little imagination to make an excellent and tasty supper dish. Increasingly there are new-fangled versions of* Flammekueche, *both savoury and sweet, but the true* Flammekueche, *prepared only from traditional ingredients and baked in the proper oven, has its defenders in the* Confrérie de la Véritable Tarte Flambée, *whose job is to ensure that this excellent dish is not traduced or misinterpreted.*

Wissembourg, right on the border, is the capital of the canton. Its Saturday market is much frequented by German neighbours in search of locally produced goods such as goats' cheeses from the Grammes farm in Lembach and Monsieur Heil's meaty *pain paysan* from Wingen. This is a favourite holidaying area, and *gîtes* and *chambres d'hôte* abound.

Lembach, on the edge of the Parc Régional des Vosges du Nord and home to the Mischler family at the Auberge du Cheval Blanc (see page 34) is the land of *la chasse*. On the main street is to be found Monsieur Richert, the butcher, known locally as Dédé. A tireless huntsman, his game terrines and pâtés from wild boar and venison shot in the nearby forests are famous, as is his *Grumbeerewurscht* (potato sausage) made from salt pork, potatoes and root vegetables, which makes a favourite supper dish. The cook has only to brush it with oil, roast it for half an hour in a hot oven and to serve it in slices with a sharply dressed salad.

On a winter's day the drive south to Strasbourg through the majestic forest of Brumath can be an unforgettable experience: freeze-dried by a stiff hoar frost, the crystal-encrusted branches of the beech trees glitter in the winter sun against a cold blue sky. Brumath's claim to fame is its autumn onion fair. In springtime a sidestep can be made to the village of Hoerdt to feast on asparagus. The Romans, original purveyors of many of the good things to eat and drink in the region, were the first to plant asparagus in the fine sandy soils of the Rhine valley. Cultivation peaked in the latter part of the last century, when the pastor of Hoerdt encouraged his poor parishioners to plant the vegetable as a valuable cash crop.

## LA CHASSE EN ALSACE

*In Alsace, shooting is strictly regulated along
German lines according to laws which
date back to the Prussian annexation in 1871.
Such tight regulation is the reason given
by many for the fairly plentiful amount of game
still to be found here. There is abundant
wild boar, roe deer and red deer, and some
pheasant, partridge and hare – though the latter
is in sharp decline due to modern intensive
farming methods. The season for wild
boar opens in April, or by special decree when
the destruction they have caused becomes
too much for local farmers and golf course
owners to bear (in their quest for food, boar tear
up whole expanses of turf and topsoil).
The season for roe deer opens in June.
A shooting permit (rather than a gun licence) is
needed for* la chasse. *Shooting areas,
owned by the village or in private hands, are let
to syndicates on a nine-year lease; leases
are bid for at auction. There are two forms of
shooting in Alsace: solitary marksmanship
from a 'high seat' in the depths of the forest,
and the more sociable* battues. *For the latter,
an area is encircled by guns while beaters
and dogs move through it and drive the
game outwards. Lunch is an important part
of the proceedings. A fire is lit in a forest
clearing, glasses are charged and the contents
gratefully gulped. To one side is a bubbling
cauldron of soup and hunks of country bread.
The hunters impale sausages and slabs of
bacon on fearsome-looking knives and grill
them over the roaring fire. Sometimes a local
group of musicians play haunting tunes on
hunting horns and older members sing wistful
hunting songs in close harmony. At the end of
the day the 'trophies' are tastefully arranged on
a bed of pine branches in what is known as
the* 'tableau de chasse'.

LEFT *The Maison Kammerzell on a corner of the cathedral square was built in the sixteenth century by a rich cheese merchant and now houses a restaurant and hotel.*
ABOVE *A little window shopping.*

ABOVE *Dinner within the cosy confines of Strasbourg's most famous Winstub, S'Burjerstuewel, commonly known as chez Yvonne after its lively patronne.*
LEFT *A wonderful window display of charcuterie at the CCA.*
RIGHT *The river Ill slides slowly past La Petite France in the heart of the city.*

# STRASBOURG

Strasbourg is the capital of Alsace, famous for its single-spired cathedral, its parliament, its shops and restaurants, its superb museums, its Christmas market. At the south-western corner of the city the river Ill opens up two arms which encircle and embrace the heart of the old town before coming together again to flow off united into the Rhine. Captured inside this area – effectively on an island – is some of the most remarkable and best-preserved architecture of the city. The names of many of the narrow streets and little squares, with their superb half-timbered medieval houses and fine Renaissance buildings, evoke an age when farmers, fishermen and wine growers would converge on the centre to sell their goods at the many bustling markets: rue du Vieux-Marché-aux-Poissons, place du Marché-aux-Cochons-de-Lait, rue du Vieux-Marché-aux-Vins.

Nowadays the wholesale markets have been banished to banal premises on the outskirts of town. Streets have been re-laid with paving stones, mosaic-style, and closed to traffic. Large underground car parks have been provided and a gleaming new tram brings visitors to the heart of town from the southern suburbs. The centre is a delight to wander in. People thread their way through the maze of little streets, pausing occasionally to press their noses against the windows of tempting shops selling foie gras, *charcuterie*, crusty white breads and dense dark loaves, fine wines and gorgeous chocolates.

At Christmas the scene is especially beautiful. Streets, houses, restaurants and shops are all decorated in exquisite taste and the place Kléber sports a spectacular Christmas tree or *sapin de Noël*. (The now widespread tradition of the Christmas tree is claimed by some to have originated in Alsace.) From early December the famous Christmas market, the *Christkindelsmärik*, takes up its position in the place Broglie and around the cathedral square. Over the centuries since the market was first instituted, the site has been changed several times but the spirit remains the same: the neat little illuminated wooden booths with their saddle-backed roofs sell candles, biscuits and all kinds of baubles to decorate the trees which are also on sale nearby. Steam from pots of mulled wine and smoke from great braziers of hot chestnuts spiral into the night sky. For complete perfection, snowflakes drift gently down and muffle the voices and footsteps of the Christmas crowd.

Strasbourg is a city of (and for) gourmets. On the rue des Orfèvres is the old-established butcher Frick-Lutz, distinguished by its quaint shop front and interior and famous for foie gras and cured meats. Around Christmas all the best butchers stock fresh goose and duck livers for making into *terrine de foie gras* (prepared perhaps at one of Christiane Bisch's cookery classes, see right), or destined for that simplest and best of Alsatian Christmas dinner openers, sliced raw foie gras seared in a hot pan and served with sautéed apple slices. Those who have neither the time nor the inclination to prepare their own can purchase the livers *en terrine* at foie gras specialists Lutz, just around the corner on the rue du Chaudron.

Seldom nowadays do you find the classic *pâté de foie gras en croûte* – a whole fattened goose liver encased in a *farce* and wrapped in pastry, resembling (in appearance) an English raised pie – which may be Strasbourg's most celebrated dish. The first of these famous pâtés was created in the city in 1780 by Jean-Pierre Clause, pastry chef to the Marquis de Contades,

## CHRISTIANE BISCH, 'LA CUISINIERE DU BAS-RHIN'

*Strasbourg, with its gastronomic reputation and cosmopolitan population, seems an obvious place for a cookery school. In 1982, in the southern suburb of Neudorf, Christiane Bisch embarked on a second career giving small, informal classes. Her guiding philosophy is that food – and cooking – should be fun. Self-taught, she decided that the best way to sharpen up her skills was to don her apron and invite herself to work for some of the principal chefs in Strasbourg and northern Alsace with whom she is on more than nodding acquaintance. In her kitchen small groups (six to twelve people) assemble around the demonstration counter to watch and lend a hand as Christiane prepares a menu of their choice. Food is seasonal, simple, chic. As far as possible, dishes are chosen that can be prepared in advance. In spite of her experience working in top restaurant kitchens, Christiane nevertheless firmly opposes the idea of trying to reproduce restaurant food at home, 'we don't have the ovens or the space or the help – and last-minute preparations are definitely not designed for home entertaining.' At the Christmas workshops students prepare their own festive foie gras. The year comes to a climax with a celebration dinner in a restaurant.*

governor of Alsace. Clause was challenged by the marquis to come up with a new and revolutionary dish as a change from what he evidently found to be an uninspired Alsatian diet. The chef rose to the occasion with the now famous dish, which found such favour that the delighted marquis immediately shared the discovery with his monarch, Louis XVI, who promptly rewarded his faithful subject with some land in Picardy. Clause received twenty pistols, married the widow of a *pâtissier* and devoted the remaining years of his life to making the famous pâtés.

Burgard (also on the rue des Orfèvres) has some of the best *bretzels* (see page 20): buy them *nature* or filled with any one of five or six fillings and eat them on the hoof – or in any case within a few hours as *bretzels* quickly stale and lose their soft chewiness. *Moricettes*, made from the same dough, are easier to fill – and to eat – because of their elongated shape, rather like an English 'bridge roll' and slower to stale because of their greater girth.

Also on the rue des Orfèvres is the pastry shop Naegel, with its bewildering choice of *gâteaux*, *tartes*, *bavarois* and ice cream bombes from the chill cabinet, as well as some outstanding *pâtés en croûte*. At Christmas it specializes in the many seasonal baked goods which are typical at this time. St Nicholas (patron saint of children, later to be transmogrified into Santa Claus) opens the season on 6 December. *Männala* ('little men'), simply fashioned, lightly sweetened figures of brioche dough with currants for eyes are made in his memory.

*Lebkuchen* or *pains d'épices* – gingerbreads variously formed, often with an icing sugar image of St Nicholas or Hansel and Gretel (a symbol of fertility in Alsace) on top – are further favourites for Advent. *Birawecka* (or *Berawecke*) is a dark, dense little bolster of dried pears, figs, prunes, apricots, apples, raisins and nuts, reminiscent (especially in its calorific content) of a British Christmas pudding. It is delicious eaten in small slices with cheese. *Schnitzwecke*, from the Munster valley, also features dried fruits (*Schnitze*) and nuts, this time wrapped in a brioche dough and baked. *Christstolle*, originally a native of neighbouring Germany, has wandered over the border and is especially popular in northern Alsace. More cake-like than the somewhat solid *Birawecka*, its dried fruits are suspended in a light sponge and the whole loaf rolled in icing sugar after baking.

Christian the *chocolatier* has two superb shops in the centre, one housed in a striking building decorated with *trompe l'oeil* and another in the rue Mercière leading up to the cathedral. A new arrival on the *pâtisserie* scene is the much-feted Monsieur Mulhaupt on the rue du Vieux-Marché-aux-Poissons, whose superb *pâtisseries* and desserts have come to the rescue of many a harassed hostess. Good bread shops abound, but Scholler on the place Broglie and Woerlé in the rue de la Division Leclerc are both specialists in the various dark breads which distinguish Alsace bakers from their counterparts in the rest of France. The best cheese in town comes from the Blondeau family, whose fine St Marcellins, Munsters and Comtés are on sale at their stall named La Fromagère at various markets in the city.

Strasbourg is famous for its restaurants. Two three-star Michelin establishments distinguish the city by their presence: Le Crocodile, owned by Emile Jung, and Le Buerehiesel, owned by Antoine Westermann (see page 32). But it is Winstubs that are really the heart of the gastronomic matter. These small cosy dining places were originally owned by wine growers and used as outlets for their products, a bit like brewers and their tied houses. Nowadays

OPPOSITE TOP, CENTRE AND BOTTOM
Delicious produce for sale at Strasbourg's
Christkindelsmärik.
LEFT A selection of Springerle, the intricately
decorated anise-flavoured Christmas biscuits.
RIGHT Lavish Christmas decorations at a
florist's shop in Strasbourg.

ABOVE AND ABOVE RIGHT Christmas
decorations in the streets of Strasbourg.
FAR RIGHT A shop front decorated like a
gingerbread house for Christmas.
RIGHT A selection of Bredele (or Bredle), which
are common throughout the Rhine lands at
Christmas time. In the old days the first
Bredele were sampled on Advent Sunday and
the rest kept until Christmas. Nowadays Bredele
are offered routinely to visitors any time from
late November until well past 25 December.

*BOTTOM AND BELOW Hops clambering up wire frames are a familiar sight on the summer skyline in northern Alsace, particularly in the richly fertile agricultural plain to the north-west of Strasbourg known as the Kochersberg. Brewing is still an important activity in Alsace and although much of the malting barley required is imported, hops are still grown locally to flavour the excellent beers for which Alsace is famous.*

the landlord is likely to be the city (Winstubs are often historic monuments in their own right) and the lease is frequently held by an enterprising chef. Most have unpronounceable names in dialect like S'Burjerstuewel and S'Munsterstuewel; others – such as Le Clou – are easier to get your tongue around.

When in Strasbourg, a visit to S'Burjerstuewel (alias chez Yvonne, after its formidable *patronne*) is a must. As you push open the door and shoulder your way through the heavy plush curtain, designed to keep out the icy winter blast, warmth and cosiness envelops you, along with enticing smells of good, simple food. The atmosphere is relaxed and friendly, the company mixed and properly democratic and the bill of fare is classic Alsace – foie gras, *choucroute, jambon en croûte, tarte à l'oignon....*

Appropriately enough for a city so closely associated with the arts of the table, Strasbourg was the adoptive home during the eighteenth century of a talented (but ill-starred) family of *faïenciers*, the Hannongs. Today the Musée des Arts Décoratifs in the Palais des Rohan on the cathedral square houses a superb collection of their earthenware and porcelain pieces. The early items of tableware by Charles-François Hannong were elegantly simple in blue and white; his son Paul made ever more spectacular use of colour and design to create works such as a gorgeous *trompe l'oeil* turkey tureen; finally, grandson Joseph succeeded in mastering the art of porcelain manufacture, and was the creator of some fine dinner services.

# THE KOCHERSBERG

To the north-west of Strasbourg is the rich farming area known as the Kochersberg. Here naked hop frames etch their stark outline against a winter sky, while in summer tobacco, wheat, barley, maize and sugar beet flourish in the fertile soil. The many fine seventeenth- and eighteenth-century farmhouses attest to the important role that agriculture has always played in the Kochersberg and to the wealth it has generated over successive centuries. Here the practice of primogeniture (unusual for France, where equal division of the spoils is the law) has enabled these beautiful farm estates and houses to be passed down intact from generation to generation. Such was the prosperity of the Kochersberg (it was known as *le grenier de l'Alsace*, Alsace's larder) that at the end of the last century it was linked to Strasbourg by tram. The traffic was two-way: the leisured townspeople soon discovered the joys of eating out in the country inns of the area, while the farmers' wives used the tram to take their produce to market, and the husbands exchanged farming gossip over a glass of wine in the city's Winstubs.

The centre of the region is Truchtersheim, where on Sunday afternoons the Maison du Kochersberg puts on exhibitions devoted to the customs, history and traditions of this farming land. Almost all the village names seem to end in '-heim', a suffix indicating Frankish origin – Quatzenheim, Willgottheim, Ittenheim, Wintzenheim and Kuttolsheim, to name the principal ones with especially imposing ensembles of farm buildings. On the northern flank of the Kochersberg is the town of Hochfelden, where the Meteor brewery (see page 29) is owned and run by the Haag family.

## BEER

*Though many of Alsace's small private breweries have been swallowed up by the big conglomerates,*
*there are still some which remain proudly independent. One such is Meteor in Hochfelden,*
*an independent Alsatian brewery, owned and run by the Haag family, which wants to remain that*
*way. In 1994 the brewery was nominated a* Site Remarquable du Goût, *an award made by the*
*Conseil National des Arts Culinaires. It is reserved for businesses which produce and sell a specific*
*gastronomic speciality in premises of special historic and aesthetic interest which can be visited by the*
*public. The firm's most famous beer is Meteor Pils, an unpasteurized beer which is sold*
*both in bottles and for draught consumption. (Meteor was the first brewery in Europe outside the*
*Czech Republic permitted to use the designation Pils, a right granted to them in 1927*
*by the then Czech administration.) Ackerland, named after a particularly lush part of the nearby*
*Kochersberg plain, comes in both light and brown versions* (blonde *and* brune *respectively).*
*Zorn Val is low in alcohol, while Klint is alcohol free. Mortimer* (pure malt) *is a beer for specialists:*
*dark, strong (eight per cent alcohol) and richly malted, it comes in casks for draught dispensing,*
*or in quarter-litre bottles complete with a chunky little whisky tumbler from which to taste it.*
*At Christmas Meteor makes a* bière de Noël, *always a little darker than the standard brew*
*and – in 1994 – subtly (and deliciously) flavoured with orange.*

*RIGHT AND BELOW RIGHT The huge cabbages known as* choux cabus *are grown extensively throughout Alsace, destined for the* choucrouterie *where they will be shredded and salted for* choucroute*.*
*BOTTOM AND BELOW At the time the cabbages are harvested, walnuts are also gathered. Local taverns offer them to be eaten with darkly smoked bacon (*lard paysan*).*
*OPPOSITE ABOVE Ready-fermented* choucroute*.*
*OPPOSITE BELOW A restaurant on the* Route de la Choucroute.

# HORSERADISH

*Horseradish is to certain Alsatian dishes as pickles to an English Ploughman's Lunch. Originally introduced into the region from eastern Europe, horseradish has come to be regarded as the condiment of the country* par excellence. *A few intrepid souls still prepare their own from grated horseradish root fresh from the kitchen garden, but many more buy it ready made by Raifalsa, a tiny family business in Mietisheim near Hagenau which has cornered the horseradish market. Horseradish is the essential accompaniment for* pot-au-feu à l'alsacienne *and goes well with all manner of smoked meats, smoked fish and game. At Winstubs (see page 26) certain dishes come accompanied by two sorts of horseradish sauce: hot, made on a béchamel base, and cold, consisting of the grated root with cream and lemon juice. Some of the area's greatest chefs have created exquisite sauces in which the fearsome bite of this rustic root is tamed by fragrant fish- and meat-based stocks and enriched with whipped cream.*

# THE PAYS DU CHOU

South of Strasbourg is cabbage country, with Geispolsheim and Krautergersheim at its heart. Here, in the autumn, tractors and trailers take their huge loads of sleek white cabbages to the various *choucrouteries* to be shredded, salted and sold for *choucroute* (see right). At this time of the year the *Fête de la Choucroute* marks the opening of the season for this robust winter dish: trestle tables are set out on the pavements and impressive quantities of *choucroute* are wheeled out, surmounted by sausages, smoked pork slices and boiled potatoes. One of the more amusing restaurants in this area is the Restaurant Schadt in Blaesheim, known familiarly as chez Philippe. Its colourful and characterful *chef-patron* Philippe Schadt is a champion of the *choucroute* cause and inventer of the Route de la Choucroute. After Blaesheim, cabbages cede gradually to vines and the wine route begins.

## CHOUCROUTE

*If foreigners – which in this context includes French people from the other side of the Vosges – attempt to pronounce the Alsatian dialect word* Sürkrüt *(the correct pronunciation is 'suerkruit') they are likely to come out with something sounding a bit like* choucroute. *The literal meaning of the word is sour (sür) cabbage (Krüt); the* chou *part of the French name also means cabbage, so* choucroute *is quite an apt rendering in French of this most Alsatian of foods. The name refers to the raw material as well as to the finished dish (*choucroute garnie*), liberally garnished with sausages, smoked meats, potatoes and (occasionally) liver dumplings. To make* choucroute, *smooth white cabbages are shredded into thin strands, layered with coarse salt in a barrel and left for a few weeks to ferment. The action of the salt on the sugars contained in the cabbage produces liberal quantities of lactic acid which serves as a preserving seal, excluding the air and enabling the choucroute to be stored for several months without spoiling. A few households still prepare their own in special barrels or crocks which are stored in the cellar but most people buy it ready fermented (but still raw) from the butcher's bucket.*

# RESTAURANT BUEREHIESEL

## STRASBOURG, TEL 88 61 62 24

*In a park in a residential part of Strasbourg close to the Parliament and the Council of Europe is a beautifully reconstructed seventeenth-century farmhouse. Originally situated in Molsheim, it was moved piece by piece to the park in 1895 for the Strasbourg Industrial Exhibition. Today it houses the Restaurant Buerehiesel (the name is a diminutive dialect word for farmhouse), Alsace's latest addition to the ranks of France's three-star restaurants. In summer, guests sip their aperitifs in the shade of the huge trees, before proceeding upstairs to be greeted by Madame Westermann. A number of intimate dining rooms lead off the main reception area, while a light and airy conservatory has somehow miraculously been suspended above the courtyard and skilfully integrated into the architecture of the original house. Antoine Westermann's food is clear, unfussy, deceptively simple, relying for its effect on the finest ingredients prepared with exquisite precision.*

# LES ASPERGES D'ALSACE ET ROQUETTE EN VINAIGRETTE AU FOIE GRAS

### *Asparagus Salad with Rocket and Pan-fried Foie Gras*

*A happy marriage of two of Alsace's most celebrated raw materials – asparagus and foie gras – with a fine bitter touch from the accompanying rocket leaves. The foie is sliced, seared and served over the fanned-out asparagus spears, dressed with the slightly sharpened pan juices. (Illustrated left)*

**SERVES 4**
**a duck foie gras weighing about 400g/14oz**
**24 asparagus spears, green or white, no thicker than an index finger**
**100ml/3 ½ fl oz chicken stock**
**½ tsp white wine vinegar**
**rocket leaves, to garnish**
**salt and freshly ground black pepper**

Using the point of a sharp knife, remove all the veins and any greenish parts from the liver. Be careful not to handle it too much, or you may find it starts to break up. Cut it into 4 diagonal slices. Refrigerate until needed.

Trim and peel the asparagus spears. Cook in boiling salted water for about 10 minutes or until they are just tender. Pull the saucepan to one side and leave the asparagus in the water to keep warm.

Heat a non-stick frying pan quite fiercely. No oil or butter is needed because of the high fat content of the foie gras. Season the liver slices and sear them briefly – about 1 minute on each side. Lift them out and keep them warm. To make the *jus*, deglaze the frying pan with the stock and vinegar, then season to taste. Strain the liquid through a fine sieve and check the seasoning.

Lift the asparagus spears out of the cooking water and split them in half lengthways. Fan them out decoratively on 4 heated plates. Place a slice of foie gras on top of the asparagus, at the centre of the fan, drizzle a little *jus* over the tips and finally garnish with rocket leaves for a light touch of aniseed.

# LA FINE TARTELETTE A LA RHUBARBE, CONFITURE DE FRAISE

## *Rhubarb Tartlets with Crème Brulée and Strawberry Jam*

*Antoine Westermann here reinterprets the perennial Alsace favourite – rhubarb tart – in personalized portions, surmounting the baked pastry with lightly buttered rhubarb, spreading it with a creamy custard and brown sugar and finally putting it under a hot grill to make the top crunchy. The dessert is free-formed at the restaurant (as shown in the photograph), but you may find it easier to serve it in individual gratin dishes. (Illustrated right)*

**SERVES 4**
**400g/14oz rhubarb**
**50g/2oz caster sugar**

**FOR THE SWEET SHORTCRUST PASTRY**
**250g/9oz plain flour**
**125g/4 ½oz caster sugar**
**125g/4 ½oz unsalted butter**
**1 egg**

**FOR THE CREME BRULEE**
**2 egg yolks**
**30g/1 ¼oz caster sugar**
**175ml/6fl oz whipping cream**
**½ vanilla pod, split in half lengthways,**
**or 1tsp vanilla extract**

**FOR THE STRAWBERRY JAM**
**300g/10oz strawberries, hulled and washed**
**60g/2 ¼oz caster sugar**
**25g/1oz unsalted butter, for the rhubarb**
**4tbsp brown sugar, to finish the custard**

Trim the rhubarb, strip it if it is stringy, and cut into 1 x 1cm/½x½in dice. Put in a mixing bowl, sprinkle with the sugar and leave it for at least 4 hours in the refrigerator.

For the pastry, mix together the flour and sugar in a mixing bowl or the goblet of a food processor. Cut the butter in small pieces and work it in until the mixture resembles fine crumbs. Mix the egg lightly with a fork and add it the flour mixture with just enough water (1-2 tablespoons) to bind it into a dough. Wrap the pastry in cling film and refrigerate.

Preheat the oven to 150°C/300°F/gas mark 2. For the crème brulée, butter a small 6cm/2½in deep, 12cm/5in soufflé dish. Beat the egg yolks with the sugar until light and fluffy. Scrape the seeds from the vanilla pod, if using. Heat the cream with the vanilla seeds, or extract, to almost boiling and pour it on to the yolks and sugar. Continue beating until just mixed, then pour into the soufflé dish and cover with foil. Place in a roasting pan or baking tin not much larger than the dish and add hot water to come two-thirds of the way up the sides of the dish. Bake for 40-45 minutes or until the crème brulée is just set. Leave to cool thoroughly, then refrigerate.

Increase the oven temperature to 180°C/350°F/gas mark 4. Cut the chilled dough in half. (The rest of the dough can be used for another dessert, or frozen.) Roll it out on a well-floured board to a circle about 3mm/⅛in thick. Transfer to a baking sheet lined with non-stick paper and bake for 10 minutes or until golden brown. While the pastry is still warm, use a 8cm/3¼in plain scone cutter to cut out 4 discs. Leave them to cool on a rack.

Cook the strawberries with the sugar for about 30 minutes, stirring from time to time with a wooden spoon. Leave to cool, then liquidize to a smooth purée. It should have a pouring consistency; if necessary, slacken the purée with water. Tip into a jug and chill.

Shortly before serving the dessert, heat the grill to maximum. Heat the butter, drain the rhubarb cubes and toss them in the butter for 4-5 minutes. Place the discs of pastry in the bottom of 4 small, 2-3cm/¾-1¼in deep, 8cm/3¼in diameter heatproof gratin dishes. Divide the rhubarb between the 4 dishes, spread with the custard and smooth the top so that it is level with the top of the dish. Sprinkle lavishly with brown sugar and put under the grill until golden brown and nicely *brulée*. Serve the tartlets with the strawberry jam, and vanilla ice cream on the side, if wished.

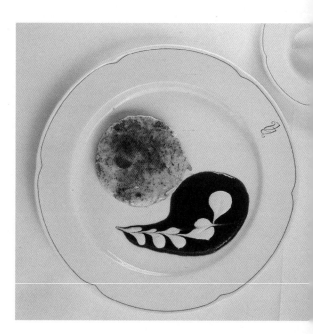

# AUBERGE DU CHEVAL BLANC

**67510 LEMBACH, TEL 88 94 41 86**

*In the days when Lembach was a staging post on the Route Napoléon from Gap to Paris, the Cheval Blanc was a post house. Owned by the Mischler family since 1909, it is now run by Fernand junior (great grandson of the original owner) and his wife Anne Marie, who earned their first* macaron *(Michelin star) in 1968 and the second in 1990. It is a big, warm house, solidly built in the typical pink sandstone of the nearby northern Vosges. Inside there are stained glass windows, big oak beams, rich plush curtains and a huge baronial fireplace. Local produce (especially game and wild mushrooms in the autumn), little echoes of* l'ancienne cuisine alsacienne, *sauces of astonishing depth and richness, and 'proper puddings' the like of which hardly anyone makes any more, but everyone loves to eat: these are the hallmarks of Fernand Mischler's cuisine.*

## FRICASSEE DE CHAMPIGNONS DES BOIS

### Wild Mushroom Fricassee

*Chef Fernand Mischler puts local cepes, chanterelles, horns of plenty and hedgehog fungus into this stew and serves it as a first course in soup bowls, or with* Rable de Lievre au Raifort *(see right). (Illustrated opposite)*

**SERVES 4 FOR A FIRST COURSE**
**6-8 TO ACCOMPANY A MAIN DISH**
**1kg/2 ¼ lb assorted wild mushrooms**
**in season**
**1tbsp groundnut oil**
**50g/2oz butter**
**2 shallots, finely chopped**
**250ml/8fl oz whipping cream or**
**crème fraîche**
**plenty of fines herbes (chervil, chives and**
**flat parsley), chopped**
**salt and freshly ground black pepper**

Keeping the types of mushrooms separate, trim and clean all the mushrooms, then slice or quarter them depending on their size. Heat a little oil to film the bottom of a frying pan and fry one type of mushroom without seasoning until they render their juice – about 5 minutes. Increase the heat to evaporate the juice, then transfer the mushrooms to a bowl using a slotted spoon. Add a little more oil if necessary and continue with the remaining types until all are cooked.

Heat the butter in a saucepan and sweat the shallots in it without allowing them to colour. Add all the mushrooms. Cook for a further 10 minutes. Add the cream and over a low heat reduce it to a syrup. Season to taste and add the herbs. Serve at once in hot bowls.

## RABLE DE LIEVRE AU RAIFORT

### Saddle of Hare with Horseradish Cream Sauce

*This excellent yet simple dish is redolent with all the flavours of northern Alsace. The same sauce would go equally well with pigeon or grouse. Serve with* Spätzle *(see page 41) and* Fricassée de Champignons des Bois *(see left). (Illustrated above)*

**SERVES 4**
**a saddle of hare (700-800g/1½-1¾ lb)**
**50g/2oz lardons**
**3 shallots, finely chopped**
**1 carrot, sliced**
**a sprig of thyme**
**1 bay leaf**
**a sprig of rosemary**
**several parsley stalks**
**1tbsp oil**
**juice of ½ lemon**
**50g/2oz clarified butter (or 2tbsp oil)**
**2tbsp cognac**

**200ml/7fl oz whipping cream**
**2tbsp creamed horseradish**
**salt and freshly ground black pepper**

Trim the saddle of any membrane, make small incisions all over and insert the lardons into the incisions. Season and put in a roasting pan with the shallots, carrot, herbs, oil and lemon juice and leave to marinate for several hours.

Preheat the oven to 200°C/400°F/gas mark 6. Lift out the meat and pat it dry with kitchen towels. Reserve the marinade vegetables in the roasting pan. Brush the saddle with the clarified butter or oil and place on the bed of reserved vegetables. Roast for 12-15 minutes – it should be just firm to the touch and remain pink inside. Lift out the meat from the roasting pan and cover it to keep warm. Discard the vegetables from the roasting pan.

To prepare the sauce, tip away any excess fat from the roasting pan, add the cognac and the cream, bring to the boil and scrape up all the residue. Add the horseradish and boil hard to reduce to a rich syrup. Check the seasoning. Slice the hare finely and serve with the sauce, *Spätzle* and mushrooms.

## SOUPE AUX POIS CASSES

### *Split Pea Soup with Vegetables and Bacon*

SERVES 4

**250g/3 ½ oz split peas
1 onion, roughly chopped
2 cloves garlic, peeled
1 bouquet garni
2 carrots, sliced
2 large potatoes, cut in cubes
250ml/8fl oz milk
100g/3 ½ oz lardons, to serve
salt and freshly ground black pepper**

Put the peas in a large saucepan with 2l/3 ½ pt of water, the onion, garlic and bouquet garni. Bring to the boil, then simmer gently for 1 ½ hours until the peas are mushy. Season to taste, add the carrots and potatoes and simmer for a further 20-30 minutes or until the vegetables are cooked. Remove the bouquet garni, add the milk and blend the soup in a blender until it is smooth.

Put the lardons in a heavy frying pan and fry gently until they are lightly golden and the fat has rendered. Toss them into the soup just before serving.

# FOIE GRAS EN TERRINE

### *Fresh Duck or Goose Liver Baked in a Terrine*

*Foie gras is a favourite festive dish in Alsace. As duck livers are smaller than goose, you will probably need to buy two to make up the weight. A thermometer is necessary to check the temperature of the bain-marie.*

SERVES 4-6

**800g/1 ¾ lb goose or duck foie gras, well chilled
2tsp (12g/½ oz) salt
½ tsp (3g/⅛ oz) white pepper
½ tsp (3g/⅛ oz) mixed spice**

Peel away any film-like membrane that encloses the liver, shave away any greenish bits and pull the two lobes apart. With a small sharp knife, make incisions down the length of each lobe to expose the main veins. Prise and lift them out carefully, taking care not to break up the livers too much. Put the salt, white pepper and mixed spice in a small dish and mix them together. Rub them well into the prepared pieces of liver. Cover and refrigerate for 12 hours or overnight.

Preheat the oven to 110°C/230°F/gas mark ¼. Pack the pieces of liver tightly into a terrine into which they will just fit, pressing down firmly. Cover with 2 layers of kitchen foil and a lid. Put several sheets of newspaper in a roasting pan and place the terrine on top. Pour in enough hot, but not boiling, water to come to within 2cm/¾ in of the rim of the terrine. Prop the thermometer up in the water to check the temperature is at 70°C/160°F. If not, place the roasting pan over a moderate heat until the water reaches the desired temperature.

Bake the foie gras for 30-35 minutes. Check from time to time to see that the water temperature is steady at 70°C/160°F, adjusting the oven temperature if necessary. When the time is up, remove the terrine from the oven and uncover it. Stick your finger right down to the bottom of the terrine. The foie gras should be barely warm and slightly melted on top; traces of blood will still be visible on the surface. Replace the lid, allow the foie gras to cool, then chill it for at least 48 hours and up to 4-5 days before slicing.

## RAGOUT DE LENTILLES AU HADDOCK ET AU RAIFORT

### *Lentil Stew with Smoked Haddock and Horseradish Cream*
*(Illustrated opposite)*

SERVES 3

**1tbsp oil or bacon fat
1 onion or shallot, finely chopped
200g/7oz green lentils
grated zest and juice of ½ lemon
3-4tbsp crème fraîche
2tbsp creamed horseradish (or to taste)
300g/10 ½ oz smoked haddock
milk just to cover the fish
salt and freshly ground black pepper
sour cream or *fromage blanc*, to garnish
chopped chives, to garnish**

Heat the oil or bacon fat in a saucepan and soften the onion or shallot without browning it. Rinse the lentils in abundant cold water. Drain them and add them to the onion or shallot with the lemon zest and juice, 500ml/16fl oz of water and some pepper and cook for about 40 minutes or until the lentils are just tender and the liquid has all but evaporated. Mix together the crème fraîche and horseradish and stir the mixture into the lentils. Add salt to taste.

Put the smoked haddock in a non-stick frying pan, pour over enough milk just to cover it and season with pepper. Simmer for 6-7 minutes. Drain the fish, then flake it and add it to the lentils. (Discard the milk, or use it to flavour a sauce.) Simmer for a few minutes to heat the fish through and allow the flavours to mingle. Check the seasoning.

Serve in soup bowls with a blob of sour cream or *fromage blanc* and sprinkle with chopped chives.

# GRUMBEEREKIECHLE AU CHEVRE CHAUD

### Grated Potato Pancakes with Toasted Goats' Cheese

*In northern Alsace potatoes are known as Grumbeere (from Grund-Beere meaning 'ground berries'), while in the Sundgau they are called Hardepfel or 'earth apples'. Kiechle comes from Küchle or 'little cakes'. In Alsace potato pancakes are often served for supper with apple sauce or a green or cucumber salad. I have combined them with grilled goats' cheese for an excellent starter or supper dish. If you prefer you can use mini-Munsters from Siffert in Rosheim instead of goats' cheese (see page 51). They also go wonderfully well with meat or smoked fish: try them with smoked salmon strips marinated in olive oil, lemon juice and some finely sliced green of spring onion. (Illustrated opposite)*

**SERVES 6**
**1kg/2 ¼ lb firm, waxy potatoes**
**1 onion, or 2 spring onions, finely chopped**
**2tbsp parsley, chopped**
**2 eggs, beaten**
**1tbsp plain flour**
**½-1tbsp oil**
**6 goats' cheeses (about 50g/2oz each) or 6 mini-Munsters**
**dressed salad leaves in season**
**salt and freshly ground black pepper**

Peel the potatoes and grate them. If you have a food processor use the grating disc. Put the grated potatoes in a bowl and season to taste. Mix the chopped onions with the parsley, eggs and flour. Add this mixture to the seasoned potatoes. Leave to rest for about 20 minutes. The potatoes will produce quite a bit of liquid.

Heat enough oil to film the bottom of a non-stick frying pan. To make each pancake, use a slotted spoon to scoop up about 1 tablespoon of the mixture, pressing down a little to extract some of the liquid. Fry the pancakes 4 at a time in the hot oil until both sides are golden; remove and leave to drain on paper towels. (The mixture should make 12 pancakes in total.) Add more oil between batches as necessary to film the bottom of the pan.

Preheat the grill to high. Transfer the pancakes to a baking sheet. Slice each of the cheeses in half to give two discs and top each pancake with one of the discs. Put under the grill for a few minutes until the cheese is melted. Serve 2 pancakes per person on a bed of seasonal dressed salad leaves.

# TIMBALES DE CHOUCROUTE

### Choucroute *Custards*

*Any choucroute left over from other recipes, such as Saumon Frais et Fumé en Croute à la Choucroute (see page 42), can be used to make these tasty little timbales; otherwise cook it from scratch (see page 43). The custards can be garnished with ham or smoked fish. Serve as an accompaniment to a ham or fish dish or with a white wine sauce (see pages 42-3).*

**MAKES 4 TIMBALES**
**100g/3 ½ oz cooked *choucroute* (see page 43)**
**2 eggs**
**200ml/7fl oz crème fraîche**
**50g/2oz ham (raw or cooked), finely chopped or 50g/2oz smoked salmon or trout, finely chopped**
**salt and freshly ground black pepper**

Preheat the oven to 180°C/350°F/gas mark 4. Put the *choucroute* in the food processor with the eggs, salt, pepper, cream and ham or smoked fish. Process roughly until just mixed. Divide the mixture between 4 buttered ramekins. Put the ramekins in a roasting tin and add boiling water to come about two-thirds of the way up the sides of the ramekins. Bake them for 35-40 minutes or until golden brown and just firm to the touch. Remove, run a knife around the edge and turn them out on to warm plates.

# GRATIN DE POIREAUX ET POMMES DE TERRE

### Baked Leeks and Potatoes with Cream

*This excellent vegetable dish can be prepared in advance. It goes with any meat dish that does not have a rich sauce, or stands on its own as a lunch or supper dish.*

**SERVES 4**
**500g/18oz sliced white of leek**
**25g/¾ oz butter**
**500g/18oz firm, waxy potatoes, peeled and thinly sliced**
**250ml/8fl oz whipping cream**
**salt and freshly ground black pepper**

Preheat the oven to 200°C/400°F/gas mark 6. Cook the leeks with the butter, 4 tablespoons of water and salt and pepper to taste in a covered saucepan over a lively heat for about 10 minutes until just tender and the water has evaporated. Layer the leeks in a buttered ovenproof dish with the potatoes and cream. Bake in the oven for 20-25 minutes until golden brown and bubbly.

# CAROTTES ET CELERI AUX PETITS LARDONS

## *Carrots and Celeriac with Cream and Lardons*

*Carrots and celeriac are cooked to crunchy-tender and combined with lightly fried lardons, onion and cream. The dish can be prepared in advance and reheated in the oven. Baby turnips could be substituted for the celeriac. These vegetables go well with chicken or other poultry dishes. (Illustrated right)*

**300g/10 ½ oz celeriac**
**400g/14oz carrots**
**1tbsp white wine vinegar**
**pinch of salt**
**100g/3 ½ oz lardons**
**1 onion, finely chopped**
**3tbsp whipping cream**
**fresh parsley, chopped**

Peel the celeriac and the carrots. Cut each of them into batons about the size of your little finger. Put them in a wide, shallow saucepan with 200ml/7fl oz of water, the vinegar and salt. Boil for 15-20 minutes over a brisk heat or until the vegetables are barely cooked and still a little crunchy and the water has evaporated. Tip them into an ovenproof serving dish. Put the lardons and the onion in the saucepan and fry gently until they just begin to take colour. Return the vegetables to the saucepan, add the cream and bring to a simmer. Stir in plenty of chopped parsley. Put them back in the serving dish. Serve at once.

Alternatively, allow the vegetables to cool in the ovenproof dish, cover them with foil and refrigerate until needed. Reheat them in the oven at 180°C/350°F/gas mark 4 for 20-25 minutes or until hot right through.

# SPATZLE

*Alsatian 'Pasta-Dumplings'*

Spätzle *would formerly have constituted a simple supper, served with apple sauce or a compote of dried fruits. Nowadays, they are more often served with meat in a rich sauce.*

**SERVES 4-6**
**300g/10 ½ oz plain flour**
**pinch of salt**
**3 eggs**
**about 150ml/5fl oz water, milk**
**or single cream, or a mixture**

In the goblet of the food processor or a mixing bowl, mix together the flour, a pinch of salt, eggs and enough liquid to give a soft, dropping consistency, like a thick cake batter. Let the batter rest for 30 minutes.

Bring a large saucepan of salted water to the boil. Tilt the goblet or bowl over the saucepan so that the batter comes just to the edge. Slice off a ribbon of batter with a sharp knife and allow it to fall into the pan. Dip the knife into the boiling water to clean it and repeat the process. The *Spätzle* will float to the surface when they are done. When there is a layer of floating *Spätzle* put the bowl of batter to one side and, using a slotted spoon, transfer the cooked ones to a bowl of cold water. As soon as they are cool, drain them and either spread them out on a tea towel, or put them in a buttered gratin dish. Do not leave them in the colander or they will stick together. Continue with the rest of the batter in the same way.

To serve the *Spätzle*, either toss them in a saucepan with hot butter until lightly golden and hot through or dot butter over them in the gratin dish and bake in a 180°C/350°F/gas mark 4 oven for 15-20 minutes or until hot.

# SAUMON FRAIS ET FUME EN CROUTE A LA CHOUCROUTE

*Fresh and Smoked Salmon with* Choucroute *in Puff Pastry*

*Here is a wonderful dinner party dish, ideal for entertaining as it can be prepared in advance ready for baking. Even those unsure about* choucroute *will enjoy this inspired combination, in which the richness of salmon is balanced by the slight sharpness of the cabbage. Serve with new potatoes and the tasty little* Timbales de Choucroute *(see page 39). (Illustrated left)*

**SERVES 6-8**

**FOR THE CHOUCROUTE**
300g/10 ½ oz *choucroute (*see page 31*)*
1 onion, finely chopped
1tbsp oil
200ml/7fl oz dry white wine
200ml/7fl oz fish stock or water
6 juniper berries
3-4tbsp crème fraîche
salt and freshly ground black pepper

**FOR THE FISH AND PASTRY**
a whole salmon, about 1.5kg/3 ½ lb, to give
about 1kg/2 ¼ lb when cleaned and filletted
or 2 x 500g/18oz salmon fillets
100g/3 ½ oz smoked salmon, very
thinly sliced
500g/18oz bought puff pastry
1 egg, lightly beaten
1 juniper berry (optional)

**FOR THE SAUCE**
1 shallot or spring onion, finely chopped
25g/ ¾ oz unsalted butter

**150ml/5fl oz fish stock, well reduced**
**150ml/5fl oz dry white wine**
**6tbsp crème fraîche**

Rinse the *choucroute* under abundant running water, squeeze dry. In a saucepan soften the onion in the hot oil without allowing it to brown. Add the *choucroute* and cook, stirring, for 5 minutes. Add the wine and stock or water, the juniper berries and season to taste. Cover and cook gently for 45 minutes or until just tender and the liquid has evaporated. Set aside and, when cool, add the crème fraîche.

Clean and fillet the salmon and remove the skin. Season the fish lightly. Roll out the pastry to a rectangle a little longer than a fillet and at least 3 times the width. Lay a fillet across one end of the pastry rectangle and spread half of the *choucroute* on top. Arrange the smoked salmon slices on top, then the rest of the *choucroute* and finish with the other fillet. Moisten the edges of the pastry and bring the other side over to enclose the fish. Trim the pastry with a knife or pasta wheel to make a fish shape. Press the edges together to seal them. Mark 'scales' with a teaspoon and stick in a juniper berry for an eye, if you wish. Place on a lightly oiled baking sheet (preferably one with a lip to catch any juices that leak during baking), glaze with the egg and refrigerate if it is not to be baked immediately.

Preheat the oven to 200°C/400°F/gas mark 6 and bake the fish on the lowest shelf (to ensure that the base pastry is properly cooked) for 30-35 minutes.

To make the sauce, heat the butter in a saucepan and gently soften the shallot or spring onion. Add the fish stock and wine and reduce by half. Whisk in the crème fraîche. Check the seasoning, adjusting if necessary.

Bring the fish to table on a board or serving dish, cut into slices and serve with the sauce.

# POULET SAUTE, SAUCE AU FOIE GRAS

*Sautéed Chicken with Foie Gras Sauce*

**SERVES 6**
**1 large chicken, about 2.3kg/5lb**
**2 carrots**
**2 onions**
**2 shallots**
**2 cloves garlic, unpeeled**
**25g/¾ oz unsalted butter**
**sprig of thyme**
**1 bay leaf**
**1 clove**
**1 wine glass of dry white wine**
**4tbsp crème fraîche**
**100g/3½oz foie gras**
**salt and freshly ground black pepper**

Cut the chicken flesh into 8 pieces, season and set them aside. To make the stock put the carcass, 1 carrot, 1 onion, 1 shallot and 1 garlic clove in a saucepan. Cover with water and simmer gently for an hour or two. Strain the stock, then reduce it by fast boiling to about 2 cups and set aside. Chop the remaining carrot, onion and shallot finely. Preheat the oven to 220°C/425°F/gas mark 7.

Heat the butter in a heavy casserole or sauteuse (with lid) and brown the chicken pieces all over. Lower the heat and add the chopped vegetables, the remaining garlic clove and the thyme, bay leaf and clove. Cover the casserole or sauteuse and put in the oven for about 15 minutes. Moisten with the wine and the stock and continue cooking for another 10 minutes until the chicken is just done. Test to see if it is ready – the juices should run clear when the thigh pieces are pierced with a sharp knife.

Transfer the chicken pieces to a serving dish and cover to keep them warm. To make the sauce strain the cooking liquid and degrease if necessary. Add the crème fraîche to the liquid and reduce a little. Off the heat whisk in the foie gras piece by piece. Do not allow the sauce to boil again. Check the seasoning and adjust if necessary. Pour the sauce over the chicken and serve immediately.

# CUISSES DE POULET A LA BIERE ACKERLAND

*Chicken in Ackerland Beer*

**SERVES 4-6**
**4 chicken legs (thighs and drumsticks)**
**100g/3½oz lardons**
**2 bay leaves**
**4 garlic cloves, unpeeled**
**3 juniper berries, crushed under the blade of a heavy knife**
**250ml/8fl oz Ackerland *brune* or dark beer**
**salt and freshly ground black pepper**

Preheat the oven to 250°C/475°F/gas mark 9. Cut the chicken legs in two and season them. Put them in a shallow cast iron casserole with the lardons, bay leaves, garlic, juniper berries and beer. Cook in the oven for 20 minutes, then reduce the oven temperature to 180°C/350°F/gas mark 4, turn the chicken pieces over and cook for another 20 minutes. Turn them again, baste with the juices and cook for a further 20 minutes. The chicken pieces should be dark brown, the garlic soft and melting inside its skin and there should be hardly any liquid left. If there is liquid remaining, remove the chicken and put the casserole over a brisk heat and boil hard to reduce to a rich caramelized *jus*.

# VINAIGRE AUX EPICES

## *Spiced Vinegar*

*Herb gardens (Krittergärtel), containing a selection of medicinal herbs (Heilkritter), culinary herbs (Kiechekritter) and decorative plants, were a familiar feature of medieval Alsace. This spiced vinegar recipe combining many of these herbs and spices can be used to make vinaigrettes or to deglaze pan juices when preparing a sauce.*

**MAKES ABOUT 1.5L/2½ PT**
**a handful each of tarragon, chervil, salad burnet, fennel and borage**
**2tbsp pickling spice**
**3 garlic cloves**
**3 shallots**
**1.5 l/2½ pt white wine vinegar**

Pick the herbs on a dry, sunny day. Put them into a clean, wide-necked glass jar with the remaining ingredients. Cover tightly and leave on a windowsill for 3-4 weeks, turning the jar gently from time to time to mix well. Strain the vinegar through a colander, and again through a muslin, nappy liner or filter paper. Pour into clean, dry bottles.

# PAIN A LA BIERE, FACON FRED

## *Fred's Rye Bread with Beer*

*Fred is the pastry chef at Le Crocodile in Strasbourg. This bread is dense and delicious, almost like a malt loaf in texture, with the characteristic slightly soapy consistency that comes from rye flour. The yeast starter is optional but speeds up the first rise.*

**FOR 2 LOAVES**
**500g/18oz strong white bread flour**
**plus 3 tbsp**
**500g/18oz rye flour**
**1tbsp salt**
**15g/½oz fresh or 1 packet easy-blend dry yeast (6g/¼oz)**
**150g/5½oz starter (*levain*) from a previous breadmaking session (optional)**
**500ml/16fl oz dark beer, preferably unpasteurized, such as Ackerland *brune***

Use a heavy-duty mixer with a dough hook to make the dough, or a large bowl and knead by hand. First of all, mix together the flours and salt, then crumble most of the fresh yeast (or sprinkle most of the dry yeast) into the flours. Mix the remaining yeast with 3 tablespoons of flour and 100ml/3½fl oz beer and set aside. Add the starter to the flours, if using. Mix in the rest of the beer and about 250ml/8fl oz of water, then work up to a dense, quite sticky dough. Knead thoroughly until it is elastic and springy, and no longer sticks excessively to your hands or the bowl. It may be necessary to sprinkle in additional flour during kneading to achieve this. Put the bowl in a plastic bag and leave to rise until the dough has doubled in bulk – about 2 hours at room temperature.

Knock down the dough and cut it in half. Flatten out each half to a circle, then bring up three sides of the circle and press them down into the middle to form a triangle. Invert the loaves on a floured baking tray and brush them with some of the yeast, flour and beer mixture. Leave to rise for about 30 minutes at room temperature or until nicely plump. Brush again with the remaining mixture.

Preheat the oven to 220°C/425°F/gas mark 7. Bake the loaves for 35-40 minutes or until well risen and a deep golden brown. They should sound hollow when tapped on the bottom.

# GATEAU CHASSEUR

## *Almond or Hazelnut Cake with Red Fruit and Meringue Topping*

*This huntsman's cake – so named, perhaps, because it formed part of his lunch, or because the red fruits that top it ripen just as the roe deer season opens – is moist and delicious.*

**SERVES 6**
**4 eggs, separated**
**150g/5½oz caster sugar**
**100g/3½oz ground almonds or hazelnuts**
**2tbsp plain flour**
**pinch of salt**
**100g/3½oz redcurrants or raspberries, trimmed**
**3tbsp slivered almonds**

Preheat the oven to 180°C/350°F/gas mark 4. Grease and flour an 18cm/7in springform cake tin and line the bottom with a disc of non-stick baking paper.

In an electric mixer, beat together the egg yolks and 50g/2oz of the sugar until thick, pale and mousse-like. The beater should leave a ribbon. Fold in the ground nuts and flour. In a clean bowl with clean whisks, beat 2 of the egg whites with a pinch of salt until they form soft peaks. Add 50g/2oz of the sugar and continue beating until the mixture becomes quite stiff and glossy. Fold the beaten whites into the yolk mixture, then turn it into the prepared cake tin and bake for 25-30 minutes or until well risen and brown, and a skewer inserted in the middle comes out clean. Spoon the fruit over the top of the cake. Beat the remaining egg whites and sugar as before and spread the mixture on top of the fruit. Return the cake to the oven for 6-8 minutes or until the meringue is lightly golden and just set.

# STRUDEL AUX QUETSCHES

## *Plum Strudel*

*This simple dessert of quetsch plums rolled up in puff (or filo) pastry is one of many autumnal pleasures at the Cheval Blanc in Lembach. There they make individual strudels, but a large one is more practical and less fiddly. Serve with vanilla ice cream. (Illustrated right).*

**SERVES 4-6**

**800g/1 ¾ lb quetsch plums (or Victorias)**
**200ml/7fl oz red wine**
**100g/3 ½ oz caster sugar**
**75g/3oz unsalted butter**
**2 pinches of cinnamon**
**1 pinch of mixed spice**
**300g/10 ½ oz bought puff pastry or 6 sheets**
**of filo and about 6tbsp oil**
**1 egg, beaten**
**3tbsp slivered almonds**

Stone and quarter the plums. Cook briefly with the wine and sugar. Lift them out with a slotted spoon, and fry briefly in half the butter with the spices. Leave them and the wine to cool.

Roll out the puff pastry to a rectangle about 30 x 40cm/12 x 16in. (If using filo sheets, overlap them slightly to achieve the same shape, brushing each sheet with oil.) Arrange the plums over the pastry, leaving a 5cm/2in border all round. Turn in the long borders and roll up the strudel from a short end, as for a Swiss roll. Place the strudel seam-side down on an oiled baking sheet. Brush with beaten egg, press the almonds on top, and chill.

Heat the oven to 220°C/425°F/gas mark 7 and bake for 20 minutes or until golden and crispy. Reduce the saved wine until syrupy and whisk in the rest of the butter. Serve with the strudel.

*RIGHT A handsome wrought-iron sign depicting a stork, the emblem of Alsace* par excellence. *In the last twenty years these magnificent birds (which were threatened with extinction) have been extensively reared locally and are once more to be seen nesting on rooftops in the spring.*
*FAR RIGHT Serried ranks of* Kougelhopfs.
*BELOW A view of Riquewihr taken from the* Schoenenberg *grand cru* vineyard.

# THE ROUTE DES VINS

*BOTTOM An old barrel serves as publicity material for a wine grower in the Bas-Rhin whose speciality is Klevener de Heiligenstein (see page 51).*
*BELOW The* alsaciens *love dancing and take to the boards at the slightest provocation. Here a local group of folk dancers entertain the crowds at one of the numerous* fêtes du vin *that take place in the villages of the Route des Vins during the autumn.*

The vineyard villages of Alsace – as any summer migrant to Riquewihr may ruefully reflect – are certainly the best known and perhaps the best loved part of the region. Each year they attract thousands of visitors who come not only to sample their most famous product but also to admire their Romanesque churches, their richly coloured half-timbered houses, their elegant Renaissance town halls and public buildings. The villages seem to be caught in a time warp, undisturbed by the passage of the centuries. Even amongst the milling hordes, a feeling of peace and prosperity prevails.

Peace is a relative newcomer to Alsace, but prosperity in the vineyards is nothing new: for centuries wine has been a mainstay of the region's economy. Vines were brought here by the Romans by a somewhat circuitous route, progressing up the Rhone valley as far as the Palatinate and then turning south into Alsace. They established themselves throughout the province, gradually covering most of the area save for the Vosges and the Sundgau.

Alsace's conversion to Christianity at the end of the fifth century brought hermits and holy men flocking to the region. Their wine requirements (both sacred and profane) gave a considerable boost to both the quality and quantity of wine growing. In 824 Ermoldus Nigellus, a poet from Aquitaine temporarily 'exiled' in Strasbourg, commented that 'the great god Bacchus inhabits these hills, grapes grow all along the mountains and wine flows abundantly. The *alsaciens* would have long since drowned in rivers of lard and wine, if it were not for the fact that the merchants export their production to the farthest shores...'

These far shores included (thanks to the good offices of the Rhine) Holland, England, Scandinavia, the Hanseatic ports, the Baltic States and Switzerland. Throughout the Middle Ages and up to the beginning of the seventeenth century, the quality and reputation of Alsace wines improved steadily. But the Thirty Years War (1618-48) put an abrupt and quite brutal end to this period of steady growth. The countryside was devastated, the population decimated: Riquewihr, for example, had 2,245 inhabitants in 1610; by 1636 it had seventy-four. With the Treaty of Westphalia (1648) at the conclusion of the war, Alsace became French for the first time in its history. The Rhine, hitherto a main artery pumping life blood into the province and communicating Alsace with the rest of Europe, suddenly became its border with a sometimes hostile state.

Almost three hundred years of gradual viticultural decline were to follow. Traditional markets were periodically closed, occupying armies came and went, phylloxera took its toll.

These were dark days indeed for the once-celebrated vineyards of Alsace. After the Second World War some far-sighted growers put into place a series of stringent measures which have enabled *l'Alsace viticole* to start its long march back to the quality levels and the reputation it formerly enjoyed.

Today, all the way from Marlenheim to Thann, not forgetting the little pocket of wine growing around Wissembourg in the far north-eastern corner (see page 22), serried ranks of regimented vines march down from the foothills of the Vosges and slope gently off eastwards into the plain. The majority of wine villages are in the Haut-Rhin, most within easy reach of Colmar. The Bas-Rhin *communes viticoles* are fewer in number and more spread out.

There is lively (and fairly good-humoured) viticultural debate between the two *départements* as to which of them makes the better wines. The Haut-Rhin enjoys all the advantages of a slightly warmer climate and produces supple, rich, full-bodied wines. (It also undoubtedly relishes the elevated connotations of the 'Haut' part of its name.) The wines of the more northerly Bas-Rhin tend to be leaner, with less sugar and higher acidity. The last word goes to Serge Dubs, *sommelier* at the Auberge de l'Ill (and a recent *Meilleur Sommelier du Monde*): '*Néanmoins, la finesse est du côté Nord...*' ('Nevertheless, the north wins on finesse...')

The interests of the wine-minded visitor are amply catered for, from signposted walking paths through the vineyards and village *gîtes* for those wishing to rub shoulders with local producers to *fêtes* galore in honour of the area's most celebrated product. Food is principally a backdrop against which fine wines can be shown at their best. Wine bars serving traditional, simple food are plentiful in the vineyards. Whilst in the north of Alsace these tend to be known as Winstubs, in the vineyards they often drop an 'n' and are called Wistubs, or even *caveaux*. There is also no shortage of restaurants, from the *grandes tables* that have made Alsace famous to simple village inns, often family owned and run. Alternatively, you can purchase a picnic, always bearing in mind that shopkeepers also like to enjoy a good lunch: the shutters come down promptly at midday, not to re-open until 2.30 p.m. Settle down on one of the benches that are thoughtfully provided at strategic intervals throughout the vineyards, and savour the moment as you survey a sea of vines to right and left.

## THE BAS-RHIN

Tracing the Route des Vins and tasting its fruits can start (or finish, depending on the order in which the task is tackled) in Marlenheim. A meal at the Hostellerie du Cerf provides a memorable introduction to proceedings. Father and son Robert and Michel Husser produce stunningly creative food (much of it inspired by their kitchen garden) in which familiar mainstays of *l'ancienne cuisine alsacienne* are given a modern twist in new and unfamiliar combinations (see recipe page 66). The village has also long enjoyed a good reputation for its red wines. Though Alsace Pinot Noir more often manifests itself as a (rather overpriced) rosé than a red, some Marlenheim growers – notably Romain Fritsch and the Mosbach family – achieve an altogether meatier result by leaving the grapes for several days in contact with the skins, followed by a spell in new oak.

ALSACE GRAND CRU

APPELLATION ALSACE GRAND CRU CONTRÔLÉE
ALTENBERG DE BERGBIETEN

Mis en bouteille à la propriété
FRÉDÉRIC
MOCHEL
VITICULTEUR
TRAENHEIM
(BAS-RHIN)
FRANCE

1994
RIESLING
12 % vol. 75 cl
Produce of France
L 342-2

# THE GRAPES AND WINES
# OF ALSACE

*The consumer of Alsace wines is spoilt for choice.
Where many wine-growing areas are restricted
to two or three different permitted cépages,
Alsace has seven: Pinot Blanc (light and zesty);
Pinot Gris or Tokay-Pinot Gris (rich and
opulent); Pinot Noir (the classic grape, usually
vinified in Alsace as a rosé); Riesling (elegant
and aristocratic); Gewurztraminer (powerfully
and unmistakably aromatic); Muscat (pure
grapes in the glass); and Sylvaner (often higher
in acidity than fruit). Edelzwicker is not a grape
variety but a blended white wine whose
composition (from any of the above) varies from
grower to grower and from year to year. Most
growers vinify all seven cépages. Some also
make Crémant, Alsace's méthode champenoise
sparkling wine. As in every wine-growing region,
one grower's wines will differ dramatically in
style from another's, even with the same cépage
grown in the same vineyard. Whatever else wine
tasting may be in Alsace, it is certainly never
boring. Labels are also informative. In the example above, Monsieur Mochel's 1994 Riesling
comes from the grand cru vineyard of
Altenberg de Bergbieten in the Bas-Rhin.*

*TOP LEFT Vineyards in the Bas-Rhin near
Traenheim. Note the mixture of fruit
trees and vines, typical of the northern end
of the Route des Vins.
TOP A grape picker delivers his precious
load of grapes.
ABOVE Grape picking is often a
family business, especially in the case of
the smaller growers.
LEFT The house of Mosbach in Marlenheim
makes a fine, meaty Pinot Noir which is
a cut above many others.
OPPOSITE A trailing vine marks the entrance
to this house.*

*BOTTOM Vineyards in the Bas-Rhin near Heiligenstein, home of the unique grape variety Klevener (see page 51).*
*BELOW The Willm family snail business in Barr. Snails are hugely popular in Alsace, sometimes gathered from the vineyards, more often tinned. They are served sizzling on the shell with the traditional garlic butter and accompanied by a crisp and nervy Sylvaner or a firm and elegant Riesling, and plenty of crusty bread to mop up the juices.*

At this northern, somewhat bucolic end of the Route des Vins, the vineyards are quite spread out and interspersed with apple and cherry orchards. Sometimes the vines are interplanted with rhubarb which casts its shady leaves over their roots. Traenheim is the home of Frédéric Mochel, one of the finest Bas-Rhin growers, responsible for some extremely distinguished Riesling and Gewurztraminer, as well as tantalizingly small amounts of Muscat: grapey, well balanced and bone dry, it makes the best appetite sharpener.

Down the road in Bergbieten the Schmitt family owns vines all around the village, about a quarter of them in the Grand Cru Altenberg de Bergbieten. A tasting chez Schmitt triggers an explosion of sensations – and of adjectives to describe them. These are wines of great class and elegance, which are to be found at the top restaurants of the region. The 'smaller' wines like Sylvaner and Pinot Blanc are to be enjoyed in their youth; Rieslings and Gewurztraminers should be kept in the cellar for several years before being drunk.

Rosheim's chief claim to fame is its Romanesque church of St Peter and St Paul, whose intriguing and humorous sculpted figures – human and animal – adorn various parts of the roof and walls. The village also has what is believed to be the oldest dwelling in Alsace, the twelfth-century Heidehüs or Heathen's House. On the road to Rosenwiller the cheese specialist Siffert sells some delectable mini-Munsters the size of small goats' cheeses, ideal for grilling and serving with potato pancakes or salad (see recipes pages 39 and 94). A steam train chugs gently through the vineyards on high days and holidays, journeying from Rosheim to Ottrott, an attractive starting point for sorties into the vineyards, the Vosges or the magnificent Mont Sainte Odile.

The tiny village of Heiligenstein gives its name to a unique wine called Klevener de Heiligenstein. Not to be confused with Klevner (a synonym for Pinot Blanc), this is made from the Savagnin rosé or Traminer grape, a native of the Jura and cousin of the aromatic Gewurztraminer, producing a wine reminiscent of but more restrained than the latter. Jean Heywang is one of the better producers of Klevener. Nearby is the somewhat sombre town of Barr, with some imposing houses, a curious museum called the Musée de la Folie Marco and a number of good food shops for picnic provisions.

Mittelbergheim advertises itself as one of the most beautiful villages in France, a brave claim given the stiff competition in Alsace alone. To judge by the large number of stone houses, the village must always have been extremely prosperous. (Stone houses were a sign of great wealth and stability, while half-timbered ones in-filled with wattle and daub were generally inhabited by people of more modest means and mobile habits. The beams could be dismantled and removed and the house re-erected in a safer place if necessary.) Many of these stone houses belong to wine-growing families, whose names are displayed in intricate wrought-iron signs, like the one outside the Seltz family property depicting harvesters on their way back from the vineyards (see page 53).

The wine traditionally associated with Mittelbergheim is Sylvaner. Ordinarily the least esteemed cépage in Alsace, yielding thin, acidic wines or bland Edelzwicker blends, this varietal has thrived since the Middle Ages on the sunny, south-facing Zotzenberg slopes above the village. Here it produces powerfully aromatic wines of unusual richness and

## ALSACE GRANDS CRUS AND LIEUX-DITS

*The* grand cru *system attempts to enshrine in law and on the label the names of vineyards whose merits had in any case been recognized – albeit unofficially – for centuries. The current tally is fifty-one, some of them truly great, others rather less so. The legislation prescribes, among other things, maximum yields (considered still too high by many), minimum alcohol levels and must weights and only four grape varieties: Riesling, Pinot Gris, Gewurztraminer and Muscat. Wines are also submitted for tasting and analysis. Grand cru wines are inevitably more expensive than 'generic' wines, and the market sees to it that the greatest of them are dearer than the lesser ones. Some grand cru vineyards proudly emblazon their names across the hillside, which helps the visitor to identify them. A* grand cru *vineyard is not an exclusive property. Vines in it will be owned by a number of growers, all of whom have the right to label their wines after the vineyard (subject to the requirements above). Lieux-dits* are 'named-site vineyards', some of which are likewise of great antiquity. Exempt from any particular restrictions (beyond those applying to* appellation contrôlée)*, the inclusion of their name on a label nevertheless suggests some unique qualities in the* terroir *that the grower wants to identify.*

complexity. Since Zotzenberg was declared a *grand cru* (and Sylvaner is not among the permitted *cépages* for such wines) many growers have grubbed up their vines and replanted with permitted varieties. Some, however, persist in making great Zotzenberg Sylvaners as they have done for centuries, and circumvent the problem of being unable to identify the vineyard if using this grape by employing cryptic language on the label: the Seltz's Sylvaner is labelled Cuvée Vieilles Vignes, while the Gilg family's is known simply as 'Z'.

Tucked up at the foot of the Andlau valley is the town which gives its name to both the valley and the river. Originally called Eleon, Andlau's old name lives on in the *clos du Val d'Eleon*, a vineyard owned by Marc Kreydenweiss, one of Alsace's innovative (and organic) wine growers. Here he produces – uniquely for Alsace – a blend of Riesling and Pinot Gris. The domaine's speciality otherwise is Riesling, particularly from the three local *grands crus*: Kastelberg (which rears up right behind the property); Wiebelsberg (next to it, towards Mittelbergheim) and Moenchberg (towards Eichhoffen).

Though Mittelbergheim may win on architecture, Itterswiller probably takes the prize for the most breathtaking position, perched on a hillside with magnificent views of the plain and the distant Black Forest. The best perch is occupied by the Hotel-Winstub Arnold, which makes another excellent base for vineyard and Vosges explorations (see page 62). Dambach-la-Ville is one of the handful of walled villages in Alsace which has remained largely

untouched by the ravages of war and planners. The main square has an imposing gabled Hôtel de Ville, several fine *vigneron* houses and the arresting Caveau Nartz, a family-run wine bar housed in an improbably higgledy-piggledy, tall, narrow building. Monsieur Dirringer, at the entrance to the village, is another grower who makes superb Muscat, one of the trickiest wines to grow in Alsace.

## FROM ROHRSCHWIHR TO AMMERSCHWIHR

Rohrschwihr was formerly celebrated for its microclimate, which made it a prime site for cherry growing. The bottom subsequently dropped out of the cherry business, but the market for fine wines such as those of the Rolly-Gassmann family continues to flourish. Marie-Thérèse (*née* Rolly) and Louis Gassmann make a formidable team: warm, generous, approachable people whose wines seem to be made in their image. Pinot Blanc in Alsace is seldom made exclusively from that grape, but often contains a proportion of Auxerrois, a softer, spicier variety which gives body and aroma to the rather lean Pinot. The Gassmanns make a pure Auxerrois, a rich, mouth-filling spicy wine of great class which is grown in the Moenchreben vineyard, and a particularly succulent Muscat.

*TOP LEFT An appealing cottage garden.*
*TOP The walled village of Dambach-la-Ville.*
*ABOVE The Seltz family's sign in Mittelbergheim*
*– note the figures on top, returning*
*from the vendanges.*
*OPPOSITE The Hotel-Winstub Arnold in the*
*town of Itterswiller.*

*ABOVE Alsace is famous for its superb geraniums and there is intense competition for the prize of* village *or* maison fleurie.
*FAR RIGHT The piper pipes his way along the road to Ribeauvillé.*
*RIGHT The Wistub du Sommelier in Bergheim.*
*BELOW The picaresque and talented wine grower Jean-Michel Deiss of Bergheim.*
*OPPOSITE, ABOVE RIGHT* Tricolores *adorn this clock tower in Ribeauvillé.*
*OPPOSITE, BELOW RIGHT This tiny walled church at Hunawihr is surrounded by vines.*
*OPPOSITE, BELOW LEFT Dancing* alsaciens.

Bergheim is a fine, fortified medieval village, outside whose walls is the Deiss family wine business. A tasting here is as much an intellectual exercise as a sensory pleasure. Monsieur Deiss is a man with a mission. Wine growing for him is a philosophy of life in which many themes are interwoven: respect for nature, a sense of holding his vineyards in trust for future generations, reverence for and understanding of the *terroir* in which his vines grow, a chafing against the constraints of Alsace *appellation* laws and an enormous impatience with wine journalists who want simplistically to label him *'l'homme du terroir'*. His wines are understated; a wine that shouts its provenance (and especially its *cépage)* to the world is, in his opinion, a tiresome, self-advertising creature. For a man who insists on the need to suffer and be subjected to stress in order to produce one's best (in the matter of vines, principally), he seems remarkably cheerful and enthusiastic about life.

Following a tasting, the intellectual theme can be pursued with a visit to the Wistub du Sommelier, where fine wines from Alsace (and elsewhere) can be sampled by the glass. These change in tandem with the specialities of the day and the mood of owner Jean-Marie Stoeckel, an erstwhile *Meilleur Sommelier du Monde*. The regular wine list (which contains thirty-three Rieslings, twenty-four Gewurztraminers and almost as many Pinot Gris) makes quite fascinating reading. The food, billed as *la cuisine alsacienne et bourgeoise d'hier et d'aujourd'hui* is simple and good.

Close to Ribeauvillé and set on a slight rise from which it commands an unrivalled view (on clear days you can see the Alps) is the home and *cave* of André Kientzler, famous for his elegant, long-lived Rieslings from Grand Cru Geisberg and Grand Cru Osterberg. He is one of the few growers in Alsace to make a pure Chasselas, an uncomplicated, thirst-quenching wine which he recommends on return from a bike ride, a favourite pastime that he enjoys with Antoine Westermann of the Buerehiesel.

Striding along beside the road to Ribeauvillé is a magnificent piper of painted wood, complete with pointed shoes, knee breeches and a feather in his cap. In centuries past pipers were among the lucky band of travellers, entertainers, acrobats and wandering minstrels who enjoyed the special protection of the counts of Ribeaupierre. Echoes of this tradition linger on in the *Pfifferdaj* (Pipers' Day), a festival still celebrated on the first Sunday in September, when music fills the streets, the fountain runs freely with wine and the *alsaciens* indulge in another of their greatest pleasures – dancing. The Pfifferhüs, or Piper's House, on the main street, one of the oldest and quaintest buildings in town, used to be a meeting place for the wandering minstrels. Nowadays it plays host to all who appreciate the traditional dishes of Alsace, which are served up in a small, cosy, wood-panelled dining room by a team of smiling waitresses. The restaurant's decorative paisley print tablecloths come from the Manufacture d'Impression sur Etoffes (Beauvillé) out on the road towards Ste Marie-aux-Mines, whose factory shop is well worth a visit.

Riquewihr is almost impossibly picturesque, the archetypal Alsace wine village whose magnificent old houses have somehow miraculously managed to escape unscathed the ravages of the centuries. The village is at its best on a mid-May morning when geraniums are just beginning to grace the window boxes, or in late autumn when a golden mist hangs over

## THE CONFRERIE
## ST ETIENNE

*Alsace's wine Confrérie is housed in the imposing Renaissance château of Kientzheim (above). Constituted in Ammerschwihr in the fourteenth century and known then as the* Herrenstubengesellschaft, *the society died out in the late nineteenth century and was resurrected after the Second World War. Its aim is to improve the quality and to promote the cause of all Alsace wines in various different ways. Chapters are held throughout the year which culminate in a dinner of great class (with wines to match) prepared by top chefs from the area. The Confrérie also holds an annual tasting of wines submitted by member growers, which are judged on their typicality and their quality. Wines achieving a certain standard are awarded a* sigille *or seal of quality.*

the Schoenenbourg vineyard, which seems to grow straight up out of the steep rooftops. The Hugel family here are renowned for their rich, beautifully structured wines, and above all for their Vendanges Tardives and Sélection de Grains Nobles (see page 59). Quieter than Riquewihr and often bypassed by the thundering hordes is Hunawihr, a gem of a village with some outstanding sixteenth-century houses. Up at the top of the village Frédèric Mallo makes elegant Rieslings (some grown in the Rosacker vineyard just below the lovely church of Ste Hune) and luscious Tokay-Pinot Gris.

As if to demonstrate the random nature of war damage, Ammerschwihr – just five minutes down the road from Riquewihr – was almost totally destroyed at the end of the Second World War. Today one can only guess at the fine houses which must once have graced the village. Famous for its grand restaurant Aux Armes de France (its chef Philippe Gaertner is one of those regularly responsible for the Confrérie St Etienne banquets, see left), it also boasts a vineyard of enormous antiquity and celebrated status, the Kaefferkopf. Traditionally wines from the four 'noble' varieties (i.e. Riesling, Gewurztraminer, Tokay-Pinot Gris and Muscat) and Pinot Blanc were grown here and vinified singly or in a blend. When the *grand cru* system was set up, growers in the Kaefferkopf had to decide if they wanted *grand cru* status (with the restrictions this implied, see page 52) or to continue as they had always done. After great debate, Kaefferkopf has now joined the ranks of Alsace *grands crus*. The most famous growers with vines in the Kochersberg are the Adam family in Ammerschwihr. Renowned for their Riesling and Gewurztraminer, they also make a superlative Pinot Blanc.

FAR LEFT *The Maison Pfister in Colmar built in
1537 for a milliner from Besançon.
The house was inhabited in the nineteenth
century by the Pfister family, hence its name.*
LEFT *The Helmstetter bakery's sign in Colmar,
depicting a* bretzel *(see page 20),
a speciality in Alsace whose shape has
been adopted as the emblem of the
corporation of bakers.*

## COLMAR

The centre of Colmar rivals that of Strasbourg for architectural beauty, but everything is on a more intimate scale. Its Musée Unterlinden (the next most visited museum in France after the Louvre), wonderful shops and markets, and its Foire au Vin each August, combine to make it a must on any Alsace itinerary; the town also serves as an excellent point of departure for visits to the vineyards of both *vignoble* and Vosges. On Thursdays a lively street market settles itself around the Ancienne Douane and in the covered market nearby, and on Saturdays it transfers to the Place St Joseph. Jacky Quesnot, the *fromager* from Buhl, is present at both, with his superb raw milk cheeses from all over France. (If you miss him at the market you may find him in his shop in the narrow, paved rue St Nicolas, see right.)

Among the town's many fine old merchant's houses are the Maison des Têtes on the rue des Têtes (now housing a Wistub and a Bourse aux Vins) and the Maison Pfister on the rue des Marchands, owned by the Muré family in Rouffach, whose stylish wines (and others) are sold here. For a wider selection of wines, especially if time does not permit personal sorties into the vineyards, La Sommelière on the place de la Cathédrale is the place to go.

Just opposite the church that houses Schonganer's exquisite painting, The Madonna of the Rose Bush in her medieval herb garden, is the baker Helmstetter, whose shop sign – a burnished *bretzel* – recalls one of Alsace's most typical breads (see page 20). Further along the street the *traiteur* and pork butcher Glasser has a veritable shoe box of a shop (the

TOP *Colourful glazed tiles criss-cross the roof of
the Ancienne Douane in Colmar.
Built largely in the fourteenth century, it
formerly served as a depot for taxable goods.*
ABOVE *The Fromagerie de St Nicolas, an
Aladdin's cave of cheese in central Colmar.*

Colmar has a colourful and lively market on the
Place St Joseph on Saturday mornings.
Most of the produce is locally grown, some of it
organic and/or biodynamic. Asparagus
(ABOVE) thrives in the sandy soils around
Colmar, most commonly the white variety.
TOP This smiling farmer's wife sells her
country breads, while a beekeeping
neighbour offers pots of local honey and
home-grown strawberries.
RIGHT A customer selects his Kougelhopf
for Sunday breakfast.

building dates from the thirteenth century) selling a gorgeous range of pies and *charcuterie* and a selection of take-away foods to make even the most motivated cook redundant. Jean, on the place de l'Ecole, is the town's favourite *pâtissier*. Chefs Michel Casenave and Christian Dosch aim to use as little sugar as possible, and to hold back on the butter and cream without compromising either the richness or the quality of the finished product.

In the heart of La Petite Venise – a picturesque old part of town through which the river Lauch quietly slides – is the Quai de la Poissonnerie where freshwater fish from local rivers and streams was sold in days gone by. To this day the Wertz family (twelve generations in the same quaint little shop since 1586) continues to sell fish here. The family business was originally founded on trade in salt herrings, which came back up the Rhine from Holland in boats which had discharged their precious cargo of Alsace wine further north. Pursuing the fishy theme, the Restaurant aux Trois Poissons (its chef an *ancien* of Tante Claire in London) serves a fine *matelote* (freshwater fish stew with white wine) and other fish dishes.

La Cotonnière d'Alsace (Paule Marrot) on the Grand'rue offers an irresistible choice of richly patterned tablecloths, napkins and curtain fabrics in both the classic Alsace paisley prints and bolder, more modern patterns. The cotton is heavy and thick, the dyes vivid and the quality outstanding. Arts et Collections d'Alsace on the place de l'Ancienne Douane sells kitchen items, decorated pottery moulds, napkins, fine linen aprons, cushions and embroidery kits, all based on original designs from museums of the area. Some of Colmar's most inventive cooking comes from chef Patrick Fulgraff at Le Fer Rouge, opposite l'Ancienne Douane, while local colour and typical dishes both ancient and modern are to be found at the Wistub Brenner in the rue Turenne and at the Caveau St Jean on the Grand'rue.

# FROM TURCKHEIM TO THANN

The final stretch of the wine road starts at Turckheim, where on summer nights the watchman does his rounds of the beautifully preserved medieval and Renaissance town centre. The bustling Auberge du Veilleur (the Watchman's Inn) serves a range of classic Alsace dishes in a kitsch-laden dining room. Wines include a good showing from the Turckheim co-operative, the best in Alsace, esteemed by top chefs, sommeliers and consumers alike.

The other famous wine name in Turckheim is Zind-Humbrecht (formerly of Wintzenheim). In 1959 Léonard Humbrecht had the great good sense (and impeccable taste) to marry Geneviève Zind. One result of the union was to combine the two families' vineyards, which are dotted about between Wintzenheim and Thann. Another was their son Olivier; the first French person to obtain his Master of Wine, he is set to follow in the footsteps of one of Alsace's greatest wine crusaders.

On the Route des Vins even chocolate seems to have vinous overtones: Grimmer the *artisan-chocolatier* in Wintzenheim makes an elegant bitter chocolate named *Grand Cru Chocolat Amer* (70 per cent cocoa), as well as a mouth-watering range of truffles, pralines and chocolate morsels of every size and shape. The shop also sells *Valrhona le Noir Gastronomie* (61 per cent cocoa), one of the finest bitter-sweet chocolates in France.

## VENDANGES TARDIVES AND SELECTION DE GRAINS NOBLES

*The designations* Vendanges Tardives *and* Sélection de Grains Nobles *are given to two sorts of wines that have been made for years in Alsace by top growers in vintages when the right conditions have been present. These precious wines range from moderately dry to intensely sweet, depending on the degree to which their (natural) sugar has been fermented out (no sugar may be added). The grapes for* Vendanges Tardives *wines should be harvested later than the main vintage (possibly as late as November or December) and may or may not be affected by* Botrytis cinerea *(the so-called 'noble rot', a mould that forms on over-ripe grapes causing them to shrivel, concentrating the sugars in them and giving these wines their characteristic richness and unique flavour). Grapes used for making* Sélection de Grains Nobles *wines may be harvested earlier or later than* Vendanges Tardives *grapes and will have been extensively affected by noble rot. In each case* cépages *are restricted to Gewurztraminer, Pinot Gris, Riesling and Muscat. Minimum natural sugar contents and potential alcohol levels are laid down by law. An intention to make either sort of wine must be declared at the beginning of the harvest, strict controls are operated in the vineyard and cellar, and the wines are tasted in the bottle at least eighteen months later.*

*TOP The little village of Eguisheim is a favourite stop on the Route des Vins. Its quaint, narrow, highly coloured houses are spread out all around the ramparts which completely encircle the village.*
*ABOVE A jovial Monsieur Théo Cattin, one of Alsace's most sympathetic and cheerful wine growers, raises a glass in front of his delivery van. The black bear of the house coat of arms depicted on the side of the van also figures on many of the firm's colourful wine labels.*

Eguisheim, built on a circular grid with a double row of ramparts, is a little reminiscent of a Russian doll: comprising a series of concentric rings, each one reveals another one hidden inside. A little tourist train takes passengers through the centre, past the mammoth wine co-operative, the Marx *boulangerie* (where the queue for fresh *bretzels* on Saturday mornings stretches down the street), the pottery shops and on up into the vineyards. On the ramparts are Le Pavillon Gourmand, serving simple *plats du vignoble* and the brightly coloured La Grangelière where the food is a little more up-market.

Oaks and peaches give their names to the village's two *grands crus*: Eichberg and Pfersigberg respectively. Two of the greatest growers in Alsace have vineyards here: Léon Beyer of Eguisheim and Kuentz-Bas of Husseren-les-Châteaux. Beyer Rieslings are elegant, understated and long-lived, their Gewurztraminers exceptionally fine. The house Pinot Noir is a particularly fruity family favourite. Kuentz-Bas wines (see page 61) are luscious, mouth filling and long lasting. Especially good are their Rieslings (from both Eichberg and Pfersigberg vineyards) and Gewurztraminers, and their Muscat is legendary.

Voegtlinshoffen is the land of Hatschbourg, a *grand cru* vineyard where Pinot Gris and Gewurztraminer flourish. In the village is the family firm of Théo Cattin et fils, famous for their massive and well-structured wines with a certain amount of residual sweetness. Monsieur Cattin is a most enthusiastic and engaging guide to the wines of Alsace, the characteristics of the different grape varieties and the history of wine growing in this area. His Hatschbourg Grand Cru Pinot Gris is particularly opulent and satisfying, while the house Pinot Noir Cuvée de l'Ours Noir (the family's coat of arms on the label is surmounted by a black bear) is a cut above most Alsace Pinot Noirs, with good deep colour and plenty of fruit. Neighbouring Gueberschwihr, with its Grand Cru Goldert, is in the heart of Muscat country. The beautiful *place* and the tiny side streets running off it are the venue in August of one of the wine road's more attractive street fairs, when local *vignerons* ply their wares to appreciative customers, and local artists show their work.

The large domain of Lucien Albrecht in Orschwihr makes award-winning and consistently fine Pinot Blancs and Tokay-Pinot Gris, while their late harvest wines are simply sublime. Jean-Pierre Dirler in Bergholtz has a number of well-placed vineyards, including several *grands crus* around the village. His beautifully balanced generic Muscat – which he opts not to enter as a *grand cru* though it comes from the Saering *grand cru* vineyard – is a blend of Muscat d'Alsace (for its floral aromas) and Muscat d'Ottonel (for finesse). After Bergholtz, the impressive Grand Cru Kitterlé vineyard breasts the hillside leading into the valley of Guebwiller, dominated by the terraced vineyards of the Domaines Schlumberger.

Thann is at the tail end of the Route des Vins. Though badly damaged in the Second World War, the town still has some great buildings, among them the *collégiale* of Saint Thiébaut with its remarkably sculpted west door. The Rangen vineyard, whose unique *terroir* and microclimate have contributed to the fame of its wines ever since the twelfth century, rears straight up from the banks of the river Thur and dominates the town. Our travels along the wine road opened with a memorable meal at Le Cerf in Marlenheim; a triumphant finale to a lunch or dinner there would be a prized drop of Léonard Zind-Humbrecht's late-harvest Pinot Gris from the Rangen, a truly great wine from one of Alsace's greatest vineyards.

## THE KUENTZ-BAS FAMILY: WINE GROWERS AT HUSSEREN-LES-CHATEAUX

*In the village of Husseren-les-Châteaux, nestling up against the foothills of the Vosges and dominated by the three towers of Eguisheim, is the Kuentz-Bas family wine business. In common with many Alsace families they trace their ancestry back to the seventeenth century when many settlers came here from neighbouring countries to repopulate the area after the devastation of the Thirty Years War. Little is known of Jacobi Kuentz, the earliest recorded member of the clan, beyond the fact that he came to Husseron from Wangen in Switzerland at the end of the seventeenth century. Three hundred years and nine generations later the Kuentz-Bas wine growing business is run by two of his direct descendants, Christian Bas and Jacques Weber. Christian is the Managing Director with special responsibility for marketing, while Jacques is the talented oenologist, responsible for the technical side of the business.*
*A small discreet sign marks the entrance to the old cobbled courtyard around which are arranged the various nerve centres of the operation – the* caveau de dégustation *(tasting room), the offices, the fine old cellars and bottling and labelling plant. At the end of the courtyard, the door to the beautiful, half-timbered Wedgwood blue family house is framed in spring by a superb wisteria. The Kuentz-Bas family owns twelve hectares of vines around the villages of Husseren and Eguisheim, some of them in the* grands crus *Eichberg and Pfersigberg (see page 60). They also rent vineyards in the surrounding areas. All seven permitted Alsace grape varieties are vinified – Riesling, Tokay-Pinot Gris, Gewurztraminer, Muscat d'Alsace, Sylvaner, Pinot Blanc and Pinot Noir – as well as some* Crémant, *Alsace's* méthode champenoise *sparkling wine.*

# WINSTUB ARNOLD

### 67140 ITTERSWILLER, TEL 88 85 50 58

*The Winstub Arnold was founded by the Arnold family in the 1960s. In the early days Monsieur Arnold and his brother (the 'Oncle Xavier' after whom some of the dishes on the menu are named) were in the kitchen while other family members served in the dining room. Nowadays the Arnolds are taking well-earned retirement and the Winstub has passed into the capable hands of the Arnolds' son-in-law and daughter, Monsieur and Madame Simon. The food is simple, strongly regional, but interpreted with a light touch and an eye to modern eating patterns. Hams are home cured and pasta is freshly made and cut by hand in the traditional way. Game comes from local shoots; traditional dishes such as* Baeckeoffe, choucroute *and* quiche *figure regularly on the menu. The façade of the building in summer is a riot of geraniums and the view from the hotel is unparalleled: vineyards, the Vosges, the Alsace plain and – on clear days – the Black Forest to the far side of the distant Rhine.*

# CIVET DE CHEVREUIL AUX CHANTERELLES

### *Venison Stew with Chanterelles*

*In Alsace the roe deer season opens in May, and this dish is on the menu chez Arnold right through the summer. Serve with* Spätzle *(see page 41) or* Pâtes Maison *(see page 73). (Illustrated opposite)*

**SERVES 6**
**2.5kg/5 ½ lb shoulder of venison (preferably roe deer)**
**50g/2oz lard or oil**
**1 carrot, finely diced**
**2 onions, finely chopped**
**1 garlic clove, crushed**
**1 tomato, peeled and chopped**
**2tbsp plain flour**
**500ml/16fl oz red wine**
**about 500ml/16fl oz beef stock**
**4 bay leaves**
**4 cloves**
**400g/14oz chanterelles, sliced**
**25g/1oz unsalted butter**
**2tbsp redcurrant jelly**
**salt and freshly ground black pepper**

Remove all skin and bones from the shoulder of venison. Cut the meat in cubes about 50g/2oz each. Heat the lard or oil in a flame-proof casserole and fry the meat in batches until it is lightly golden, removing the cubes as they are ready. In the same fat, soften the carrot, onions, garlic and tomato. Sprinkle on the flour and cook until it colours a little. Return the meat to the casserole. Preheat the oven to 150°C/300°F/gas mark 2. Add the wine and enough stock to cover the meat comfortably. Stir well, season to taste, add the bay leaves and cloves, cover and simmer in the oven for about 1 ½ hours until just tender.

Heat the butter in a frying pan and fry the chanterelles for about 10 minutes, then season to taste. When the meat is tender, strain it over a bowl and degrease the juice carefully with paper towels. To make the sauce, whisk the redcurrant jelly into the juice and check the seasoning. Return the meat to the casserole, pour over the sauce and add the chanterelles. Simmer for a minute or so to heat through.

## MOUSSES AUX MIRABELLES

### *Mirabelle Mousses*

*Mirabelles are damson-sized sweet yellow plums with a delicate pinkish blush. If you cannot find mirabelles, use greengages or Victoria plums instead. (Illustrated above)*

**SERVES 4**
**1 sheet of gelatine or ½ tsp**
**powdered gelatine**
**2 egg yolks**
**250g/8 ½ oz strained mirabelle pulp (frozen or tinned)**
**100ml/3 ½ fl oz double or whipping cream**

Soak the gelatine sheet in cold water until it is floppy, then squeeze it out, or soak the powered gelatine in 1 tablespoon of water until spongy. Put the egg yolks in a saucepan. Heat the mirabelle pulp in a second saucepan and pour it on to the yolks. Beat vigorously over a gentle heat until somewhat thickened. Do not allow to boil. Remove from the heat, add the sheet of gelatine or powdered gelatine and stir until it has dissolved. Allow to cool.

Whip the cream and fold it into the purée. Divide the purée between 4 lightly oiled ramekins and chill until firm.

# ZUM PFIFFERHUS

**68150 RIBEAUVILLE, TEL 89 73 62 28**

*On the main street of Ribeauvillé, this little old half-timbered house with its listed fourteenth-century façade is a favourite Wistub for off-duty chefs and local viticulteurs – there's often a Trimbach tucked away in a corner somewhere. Chef-patron Laurent Meistermann, a native of the Munster valley, trained first as a boucher-charcutier, then as a chef in various restaurants in Paris before returning to the vineyards in 1973 to take over the historic Wistub zum Pfifferhüs. His is traditional, tasty Alsatian cuisine which he has re-created and allégée (lightened). His menu includes dishes such as a salad of blanched choucroute garnished with slivers of smoked goose breast or fillets of trout with a sauce of crémant d'Alsace. All charcuterie is – as you would expect from a professional charcutier – home made, and a superb selection of delicious fruit tarts sits alluringly on the dark wood counter.*

## KASSLER EN CROUTE

*Smoked Pork Loin in a Pastry Crust*

(Illustrated right)

**SERVES 6**
**1 egg, lightly beaten**
**½ wine glass of dry white wine**
**300g/10 oz finely ground sausagemeat (preferably pork and veal)**
**800g-1kg/1 ¾ -2 ¼ lb piece of smoked pork loin**
**500g/18oz bought puff pastry**
**1 egg, to glaze**

Work the egg and wine into the sausagemeat by hand or in the food processor until thoroughly mixed. Roll out the pastry to a large rectangle that is at least twice the width and a little longer than the pork, about 30 x 50cm/12 x 20in. Cut off a narrow strip of pastry from the width and reserve. Spread the sausagemeat mixture onto about two-thirds of the surface of the pastry, without going to the edges, and place the pork in the middle. Paint the edges of the pastry with water and then bring the sides of the pastry up and over the meat to enclose it completely. Press the edges and the seam to form a good seal. Brush with beaten egg and lay the reserved strip of pastry on top to make a 'hat'. Make incisions in the pastry and decorate with any trimmings. Chill the dish if it is not to be baked immediately.

Preheat the oven to 220°C/425°F/gas mark 7. Bake for 10-15 minutes, then reduce the oven temperature to 180°C/350°F/gas mark 4 and bake for a further hour.

## KOUGELHOPF

*Sweet Loaf with Raisins and Almonds*

**SERVES 6-8**
**500g/18oz strong white bread flour**
**1tsp salt**
**4tbsp sugar**
**1 packet (6g/ ¼ oz) easy-blend dry yeast or 15g/ ½ oz fresh yeast**
**200ml/7fl oz warm milk**
**2 eggs**
**125g/4 ½ oz butter, soft but not melted**

**75g/3oz sultanas or seedless raisins,
rolled in flour and shaken out
in a colander
as many almonds as there are runnels in
the *Kougelhopf* mould
icing sugar, for dusting**

With the dough hook of the electric mixer fitted, mix together the flour, salt, sugar and dry yeast. (If using fresh yeast, dissolve it in a little of the milk and add to the rest of the milk.) Mix the milk with the eggs, then add to the flour mixture, together with the butter. Work in, then beat thoroughly for at least 10 minutes until the mixture comes away from the sides of the bowl. It will remain quite soft, rather like a cake batter. Press your knuckles into it. Encase the bowl in a plastic bag and allow the dough to rise at room temperature for 1-1½ hours, or until doubled in bulk.

When the dough has risen, knock back and work in the floured sultanas or raisins. Butter a 1.75l/3pt *Kougelhopf* mould. Put an almond in each runnel. Using a dough scraper, lift the dough out of the bowl and press it down into the runnels. Leave to rise at room temperature.

Preheat the oven to 180°C/350°F/gas mark 4. When the dough has risen until it almost reaches the rim of the mould, put in the oven and bake for 40-45 minutes or until well risen and golden brown. Invert onto a rack to cool. Sprinkle with icing sugar before serving.

Serve slices, fried in butter, with *crème anglaise* for a delicious dessert.

## SALADE DE MACHES DES VIGNES AU FOIE GRAS DE CANARD

### *Wild Lamb's Lettuce and Mushroom Salad with Warm Foie Gras*

*A wonderful starter from chef Michel Husser at the Hostellerie du Cerf in Marlenheim. Lamb's lettuce grows wild throughout the vineyards of Alsace. If truffles are in short supply, they can be omitted. (Illustrated left)*

**SERVES 6**

**FOR THE VINAIGRETTE**
**3tbsp balsamic vinegar**
**1tbsp lemon juice**
**1tbsp sherry vinegar**
**5tbsp chicken stock**
**225ml/7 ½ fl oz olive oil**
**salt and freshly ground black pepper**

**FOR THE SALAD**
**1tbsp olive oil**
**1 shallot, finely chopped**
**300g/10oz mixed wild mushrooms such as chanterelles, horns of plenty and ceps**
**300g/10oz lamb's lettuce**
**350g/12oz duck foie gras**

**FOR THE TRUFFLE GARNISH (OPTIONAL)**
**15g/ ½ oz truffle**
**100ml/3 ½ fl oz port**
**100ml/3 ½ fl oz cognac**
**100ml/3 ½ fl oz veal stock**

Mix together all the ingredients for the vinaigrette in the blender. If using truffle, chop it finely and cook it very gently in the port, cognac and veal stock for 5-6 minutes.

Heat the oil in a saucepan and gently soften the shallot, then add the trimmed and sliced mushrooms. Cover and cook gently for 5 minutes until the juices are rendered. Uncover and raise the heat to concentrate and evaporate the juices. Sprinkle the mushrooms with 2-3 tablespoons of the vinaigrette.

Toss the lamb's lettuce in some more of the vinaigrette and arrange it on 6 plates. Put a mound of mushrooms in the middle of each plate. Slice the foie gras in 6 slices and season them. Heat a non-stick frying pan quite fiercely and sear the slices briefly till just golden – about a minute or so on each side. Place one slice on each of the salads. If you are using truffle, scatter it on top of the salad and drizzle the cooking juices around the edge of the salads. Serve at once.

## SALADE VIGNERONNE

*Salad of Smoked Sausage, Cheese, Onion and Tomatoes*

*In former times this rich and robust salad was served as the starter before* choucroute garnie *(see page 31). Nowadays, with our more modest appetites, most people find it is quite a meal in itself. Alsatian* cervelas *(saveloys) are short, stubby, smoothly textured, lightly smoked sausages made from pork and beef. They can simply be skinned and eaten in a salad because they are already cooked.*

**SERVES 6**
**FOR THE VINAIGRETTE**
**1 tbsp mustard**
**300ml/10fl oz oil**
**100ml/3 ½ fl oz vinegar**
**1 egg, hard-boiled**
**salt and freshly ground black pepper**

**FOR THE SALAD**
**6 cervelas**
**3 shallots, finely chopped**
**300g/10 ½ oz Gruyère cheese,**
**coarsely grated**
**cornichons or radishes, chopped**
**a selection of mixed salad leaves such as**
**green and red oakleaf, cos, lollo rosso**
**and radicchio**
**large bunch of parsley, chopped**
**6 tomatoes, cut in quarters, to garnish**

Blend the mustard, oil, vinegar, yolk of the hard-boiled egg and the salt and pepper together in a liquidizer till smooth.

Skin the sausages and cut in matchstick strips or slices. Mix with the shallots, Gruyère, chopped egg white and cornichons or radishes and some of the dressing in a large bowl. Toss the salad leaves in a little vinaigrette to coat, then arrange them on 6 plates. Divide the sausage and cheese salad between the plates, sprinkle with chopped parsley and garnish with tomato quarters.

## AUMONIERES DE CHAMPIGNONS ET D'ESCARGOTS, SAUCE CIBOULETTE

*Brik Pastry Parcels with Mushrooms and Snails with a Chive Sauce*

*In Alsace there is a large immigrant population from the Maghreb. They have introduced brik pastry leaves (*feuilles de brik*) into the region. The brik pastry leaves are like superfine crêpes (which are a good alternative) and are now made locally.*

**SERVES 6**
**1 shallot, finely chopped**
**2 garlic cloves, crushed**
**1 tbsp oil**
**350g/12oz wild or cultivated mushrooms,**
**sliced or quartered**
**300ml/10fl oz crème fraîche**
**3 dozen tinned snails (medium size)**
**150ml/5fl oz chicken stock**
**150ml/5fl oz dry white wine**
**6 brik leaves or 6 crêpes (see page 94) about**
**20cm/8in diameter**
**oil for brushing**
**plenty of chopped chives**
**salt and freshly ground black pepper**

Heat the oil in a large frying pan and gently soften the shallot and garlic without allowing them to colour. Add the mushrooms and season to taste. Cover with a lid or foil and cook gently until the mushrooms render their juices – this should take about 10 minutes. Uncover and cook hard to evaporate the juices. Stir in 3-4 tablespoons of crème fraîche to bind. Set aside.

Rinse the snails well. Simmer them in the stock and wine for 10 minutes with salt and pepper to taste. Lift them out with a slotted spoon and add them to the mushrooms. Reserve the cooking liquid.

Preheat the oven to 200°C/400°F/gas mark 6. Place a heap of filling in the middle of each brik leaf or crêpe, bring the edges up over the filling to make a parcel, and place the parcels seam-side down on an oiled baking sheet. Brush the pastry with oil and bake towards the top of the oven for 10-12 minutes or until golden brown and crispy.

Meanwhile make the sauce. Reduce the snail cooking liquid by half, then whisk in the remaining crème fraîche. Remove from the heat and stir in the chives.

## HARENGS MARINES A LA CREME

### Marinated Herring Fillets, Apples and Onions with Sour Cream

Herrings have played an important part in the Alsace diet for several centuries and formerly constituted one of the province's staple foods. They came principally from Holland – in the Middle Ages the boats which carried Alsace wine down the Rhine to the Low Countries were loaded for their return with a cargo of herrings. The combination of apple and fish fillets in a sharp creamy marinade is typical of the Alsatian fondness for the sweet-sour element in dishes. Serve with good wholewheat bread and/or new potatoes in their skins

**SERVES 4-6**
**400g/14oz sweet-cured herring fillets**
**milk for soaking herring fillets**
**2 small onions, cut into thin rings**
**½ Granny Smith apple, cored and cut into thin slices**
**100ml/3½ fl oz white wine vinegar**
**200ml/7fl oz sour cream or crème fraîche**
**freshly ground black pepper**

Separate the herring fillets and put them in a wide, shallow dish. Cover with milk and leave for several hours in order to draw out excess salt. Remove the fillets and pat dry with paper towels. Put a layer of the fillets in a small dish or terrine, add pepper to taste, some onion rings and slices of apple. Repeat the layers until all the ingredients are used up. Finish by pouring over the vinegar and then the sour cream or crème fraîche.

Cover with cling film and leave to marinate for at least 24 hours. They will keep for up to 5 days in the fridge.

## QUICHE AUX CHAMPIGNONS A L'ALSACIENNE

### Mushroom and Tomato Quiche

Another favourite Winstub dish, this excellent quiche is ideal for either lunch or supper, served with a salade de saison. Chopped ham, smoked or unsmoked, makes a tasty addition. Tarragon is nice in summer; in winter nutmeg makes a good flavouring.

**SERVES 6-8**
**FOR THE PASTRY**
**200g/7oz plain flour**
**50g/2oz salted butter**
**50g/2oz margarine**
**pinch of salt**

**FOR THE FILLING**
**25g/1oz butter**
**2 shallots, finely chopped**
**2 tomatoes, peeled, deseeded and chopped**
**500g/18oz mushrooms, sliced**
**2tbsp tarragon, chopped, or ¼ tsp grated nutmeg**
**250ml/8fl oz cream**
**100ml/3½ fl oz milk**
**3 eggs**
**100g/3½ oz ham (cooked or raw smoked), diced, optional**
**salt and freshly ground black pepper**

Make up the pastry with the flour, salt, butter, margarine and iced water according to your own preferred pastry method, or as instructed on page 69. Wrap it in cling film or foil and then refrigerate.

Heat the butter in a large, wide saucepan and gently soften the shallots in it without allowing them to brown. Raise the heat, add

the tomato flesh and cook, stirring, until the juices have evaporated a little. Add the mushrooms to the saucepan, season to taste and flavour with tarragon or nutmeg. Cover the saucepan and cook gently for 10 minutes until the mushroom juices are rendered. Uncover and cook hard for a further 5 minutes to evaporate and concentrate the juices. Set aside to cool. Mix together the cream, milk and eggs, then stir in the cooled mushroom mixture and ham (if used). Check the seasoning and chill the filling if not to be used immediately.

**SERVES 4-6**
**FOR THE PASTRY**
200g/7oz plain flour
100g/3½oz salted butter

**FOR THE FILLING**
500g/18oz onions, finely sliced
50g/2oz butter
a pinch of nutmeg
2tbsp flour
150ml/5fl oz cream
150ml/5fl oz milk
3 eggs, lightly beaten
salt and freshly ground black pepper
100g/3½oz lardons, optional

Put the flour in a mixing bowl or the goblet of a food processor. Cut the butter into small pieces and work it in until the mixture resembles fine crumbs. Add 7 teaspoons of iced water and mix until the dough forms a bowl. Wrap in cling film and refrigerate.

Preheat the oven to 200°C/400°F/gas mark 6. Roll out the pastry to fit a 26cm/10¼in loose-bottomed quiche tin. In a frying pan heat the butter and very gently soften the onions in it with salt, pepper and nutmeg to taste. Stir the mixture from time to time. Do not hurry this operation: the onions should cook slowly to a rich golden colour. Sprinkle on the flour and cook for 5 minutes, stirring constantly. Add the cream and milk and bring to the boil, still stirring the mixture, then simmer gently for 5 minutes. Take off the heat and stir in the eggs.

Tip the filling into the pastry case and sprinkle with the lardons, if using. Bake for 15 minutes on a preheated baking sheet on the lowest shelf of the oven, then reduce the oven temperature to 180°C/350°F/gas mark 4 and move the quiche up a shelf. Bake for a further 20-25 minutes until golden brown and set.

# TARTE A L'OIGNON

## *Onion Tart*

*This classic Alsace recipe consists of a golden onion ointment lightly bound with flour, milk, cream and eggs. If you have a solid fuel or an electric oven, start the quiche off on the floor of the oven to ensure that the pastry base is cooked through. Otherwise bake the quiche on a black baking sheet that has been preheated in the oven (see left). (Illustrated above)*

Preheat the oven to 200°C/400°F/gas mark 6 and place a baking sheet on the lowest shelf of the oven, or on the floor of a solid fuel or electric oven to get thoroughly hot. Roll out the pastry to line a 26cm/10¼in loose-based quiche tin. Pour the filling into the pastry case, put the quiche on the preheated baking sheet and bake for 15 minutes. Move the quiche up a shelf, lower the temperature to 180°C/350°F/gas mark 4 and bake for a further 25-30 minutes or until the filling is golden brown and set.

# TERRINE LEGERE AU GEWURZTRAMINER

*Light Terrine of Poultry Breast and Pork with Gewurztraminer*

**SERVES 10-12**
**500g/18oz skinless, boneless chicken or turkey breasts**
**500g/18oz neck of pork**
**1 garlic clove, crushed**
**1 onion, finely chopped**
**1 shallot, finely chopped**
**1 carrot, coarsely grated**
**freshly ground nutmeg**
**¼ bottle Gewurztraminer (or other strongly aromatic, slightly sweet white wine)**
**plenty of freshly chopped *fines herbes* such as parsley, chervil and chives**
**150g/5oz pure pork sausagemeat**
**1 bouquet garni**
**thin slices of streaky bacon or back fat**
**salt and freshly ground black pepper**

Using a very sharp knife, finely chop the chicken or turkey breasts and the pork. Put the chopped meat in a large bowl with the garlic, onion, shallot, carrot, nutmeg, and salt and pepper to taste. Add the wine, mix well, cover and chill the mixture for at least 12 but not longer than 24 hours.

The next day, lift out the meats using a slotted spoon. Reserve the marinade. Mix the herbs into the sausagemeat and season to taste. Lay the bouquet garni in the bottom of a 8cm/3in deep, 26 x 10cm/10¼ x 4in terrine or loaf tin, then line it with slices of bacon or back fat, reserving some slices for the top. Layer the sausagemeat with the marinated meat. Pour on the reserved marinade. Finish with the remaining bacon or back fat slices, a double layer of foil and a lid.

Preheat the over to 180°C/350°C/gas mark 4. Put some sheets of newspaper in a roasting pan and put the terrine on top. Add water to come to within about 2cm/¾in of the top of the terrine. Bring the water almost to a simmer on top of the stove, then carefully transfer to the oven and bake for 1½-2 hours or until firm to the touch, the juices are clear and the terrine has slightly shrunk from the sides.

Leave the terrine to cool, then put a weight on top and chill until serving time.

# GRATIN DE POMMES DE TERRE ET CELERI AU VIN BLANC D'ALSACE

*Potato and Celeriac Gratin with White Wine and Butter*

**SERVES 4**
**2 onions, finely sliced**
**75g/3oz butter**
**500g/18oz firm, waxy potatoes, peeled and thinly sliced**
**500g/18oz celeriac, peeled and thinly sliced**
**150ml/5fl oz dry white wine**
**150ml/5fl oz stock**
**salt and freshly ground black pepper**

Preheat the oven to 200°C/400°C/gas mark 6. Fry the onions until lightly golden in a knob of the butter. Layer them with the potatoes and celeriac in a shallow, buttered ovenproof dish with the rest of the butter, cut in pieces. Season as you go. Heat the wine and stock and pour it over. Bake in the oven for 45-50 minutes or until the top is golden brown and crusty, the vegetables are cooked and the liquid has evaporated.

# CAILLES A LA VIGNERONNE

*Quail Stuffed with Goats' Cheese with a Creamy Grape Sauce*

*(Illustrated opposite)*

**SERVES 3-6**
**6 quail**
**6 small fresh goats' cheeses (15g/½oz each) or 6 slices of *chèvre bûche***
**15-25g/½-1oz butter**
**1-2tbsp oil**
**2 shallots, finely chopped**
**200ml/7fl oz dry white wine such as Riesling**
**2tbsp *marc d'Alsace* (or Cognac), optional**
**4-5tbsp crème fraîche**
**150g/5oz white table grapes, halved and pipped**
**salt and freshly ground black pepper**
**vine leaves, to garnish, optional**

Season the quails inside and out and put a whole or slice of goats' cheese inside each bird. Heat half the butter and 1 tablespoon of oil in a wide saucepan equipped with a lid, put in the birds and brown them all over. Remove them and cover to keep warm. Discard the fat if it has burnt and replace it with new. Soften the shallots without allowing them to colour. Deglaze the saucepan with the wine and *marc* or Cognac, if using. Return the birds to the saucepan, bring to the simmer, cover and cook very gently for 10 minutes.

Lift out the birds and cover to keep warm. Whisk the crème fraîche into the juices in the saucepan and add the grapes. Simmer gently to heat the grapes through. Arrange the birds on a warm serving dish or individual plates, spoon over the sauce, garnish with vine leaves and serve at once.

# POULET AU RIESLING

## *Chicken in White Wine Cream Sauce with Mushrooms*

*One of the simplest and best of Alsace recipes. The original recipe calls for a tasty young cockerel, but a large, free-range chicken will do instead. This dish is often served with* Pâtes Maison *(see right). (Illustrated opposite)*

**SERVES 4-6**
**a 1.5kg/3 ½ lb chicken, cut in 8 pieces**
**flour for coating**
**50g/2oz butter**
**2tbsp oil**
**2 shallots, finely chopped**
**1 garlic clove, crushed**
**2tbsp Cognac or *eau-de-vie*, optional**
**250ml/8fl oz Riesling or other dry**
**white wine**
**250ml/8fl oz chicken stock**
**1 bouquet garni**
**100ml/3 ½ fl oz crème fraîche**
**150g/5oz mushrooms, sliced**
**salt and freshly ground black pepper**

Season the chicken pieces and toss lightly in flour. Heat half the butter and half the oil in a large heavy saucepan and fry the chicken pieces on all sides until lightly golden. Remove them and soften the shallots and garlic in the same fat. Add the Cognac or *eau-de-vie* and flambé, if using. Return the chicken to the saucepan, add the wine, stock and bouquet garni. Cover and simmer very gently for 40-45 minutes or until just done. To test, stick a skewer into the fattest part of the thigh – the juices should run clear. Lift out the chicken pieces and cover to keep warm. Reduce the cooking juices by half, whisk in the crème fraîche and simmer a further 5 minutes.

Fry the mushrooms in the remaining butter and oil. Put the chicken pieces back into the sauce and add the mushrooms. Stir well to blend and reheat thoroughly before serving.

# PATES MAISON

## *Home-made Ribbon Noodles*

*It comes as a surprise to many that the alsaciens love pasta, eating it frequently with fish, poultry, meat or by itself. They often make their own pasta, which they announce with pride as* 'salbschtg'machti Nüdle' *(home-made noodles). A food processor is ideal for making the dough. (Illustrated opposite)*

**SERVES 6**
**3 eggs, lightly beaten**
**300g/10oz strong white bread flour**
**1tsp salt**
**a little oil if necessary**

Mix the eggs into the flour and salt either in a food processor or a mixing bowl to make a firm dough. If necessary, add a little oil. Knead well until very elastic. Rest the dough, covered with cling film, for at least 1 hour. On a lightly floured board, roll the dough out as thinly as possible to a large rectangle. To prepare the pasta sheet for cutting, flour the top of it well, then fold it over and over on itself as if making a roulade. Slice the pasta into ribbons of the desired width, then shake them out on the board to separate them. Cook in abundant boiling salted water for 2-3 minutes – tasting frequently to see if they are done. For a typical Alsace touch keep back a small handful of raw noodles and toss them in hot oil for a few minutes until golden. Scatter over the cooked noodles before serving.

## TARTE AUX RAISINS ET AUX NOIX

### Grape Tart with Fresh Walnuts

*This lovely dessert is often served during the vendanges, when grapes and fresh walnuts are plentiful. The best grapes to use are the thin-skinned Muscat or Chasselas. (Illustrated above)*

**SERVES 6**
**FOR THE PASTRY**
**100g/3½ oz salted butter**
**200g/7oz plain flour**
**1kg/2¼ lb Muscat or Chasselas grapes,**
**pips removed**

**2tbsp *marc d'Alsace* or other *eau-de-vie***
**75g/3oz sugar**
**100g/3½ oz ground walnuts (or almonds)**
**5tbsp milk**
**5tbsp crème fraîche**
**3 eggs**
**icing sugar, optional**

Macerate the grapes in the *marc* or other spirit and the sugar for several hours.

Put the flour in a mixing bowl or the goblet of a food processor. Cut the butter into small pieces and work it in until the mixture resembles fine crumbs. Add 7 teaspoons of iced water and mix until the dough forms a ball. Wrap in cling film and refrigerate.

Heat the oven to 200°C/400°F/gas mark 6. Roll out the pastry to line a 26cm/10¼ in loose-bottomed quiche tin or 6 patty tins. Prick the pastry, weight it down with foil and baking beans, then bake blind for 7-10 minutes. Remove the foil and beans and return to the oven for 3-5 minutes or until lightly golden.

Scatter the nuts over the pastry. Put the grapes in a strainer and shake, reserving the juice. Arrange the grapes on top of the nuts. Whisk the juice together with the milk, crème fraîche and eggs until thick and mousse-like. Spoon the mixture over the grapes. Bake the individual tarts for 15-20 minutes, or the large tart for 30-35 minutes, until golden brown. Cool on a rack and sprinkle with icing sugar.

# SOUPE DE PECHES DE VIGNE AU MUSCAT ET A LA MENTHE

## *Iced Peach Soup with Muscat and Mint*

*Peaches – especially the tiny, intensely flavoured, red-fleshed pêches de vigne – are sometimes grown in the vineyards of Alsace. For lack of pêches de vigne, use ordinary peaches or nectarines and serve one each, cut in half. (Illustrated opposite)*

### SERVES 6
**12 *pêches de vigne* or 6 cultivated peaches or nectarines**
**125ml/4fl oz Muscat d'Alsace**
**juice and zest of 1 orange**
**juice and zest of 1 lemon**
**75g/3oz sugar**
**several sprigs of mint**
**a handful of wild strawberries, optional**

Cover the peaches with boiling water, leave for 1-2 minutes, then remove the skins. (Nectarines need not be peeled.) If they can easily be halved and stoned, do this; it makes them easier to eat, otherwise leave whole. Put the fruit in a wide deep bowl in which they will fit in one layer, with room for the syrup. Pour over the Muscat, orange and lemon juice. Simmer together 300ml/10fl oz of water, the sugar, the mint (set aside a small sprig for decoration) and some fingernail-sized pieces of orange and lemon zest until the sugar dissolves. Pour this hot syrup over the peaches to cover them completely and leave to infuse for several hours or overnight. Serve well chilled with mint leaves floating on top and decorate with wild strawberries, if available.

# LE GATEAU AU CHOCOLAT DU SOMMELIER

## *The Sommelier's Chocolate Cake*

*This sinfully rich chocolate cake comes from the Wistub du Sommelier in Bergheim. Its quality hinges entirely on the calibre of chocolate used, which should contain at least 52 per cent cocoa solids. The icing is a silky smooth layer of melted chocolate and cream.*

### SERVES 8-10
**FOR THE SPONGE CAKE**
**4 eggs**
**175g/6oz sugar**
**50g/2oz flour, sifted**
**100g/3 ½ oz butter**
**100g/3 ½ oz best-quality dark chocolate**
**2tbsp Cointreau or Grand Marnier**

**FOR THE ICING**
**100g/3 ½ oz best-quality dark chocolate**
**100ml/3 ½ fl oz single cream**
**coffee beans, shaved chocolate or wild strawberries, to decorate**

Preheat the oven to 180°C/350°F/gas mark 4. Butter and flour the sides of a 22cm/8 ¾ in springform cake tin and line the bottom with a disc of non-stick baking paper. In the electric mixer, beat together the eggs and sugar until thick, pale and mousse-like and the mixture has at least tripled in bulk. Sprinkle on the sifted flour and, using a balloon whisk, lift and fold the flour delicately into the egg mixture. Melt the butter and chocolate in a heavy-based saucepan over a very gentle heat, stirring occasionally until smooth and glossy. Dribble it carefully down the side of the bowl containing the sponge mixture and lift and fold it into the mixture. Turn the mixture into the prepared cake tin and bake for 35 minutes or until the top is just firm and a skewer inserted in the middle comes out clean. Cool on a rack for 5 minutes then drizzle over the Cointreau or Grand Marnier. When cold, release the spring-form. The cake will sink somewhat.

To make the icing, melt the chocolate in the cream in a heavy-based saucepan over a low heat. Allow it to cool, then beat thoroughly with an electric mixer until smooth. Spread the icing over the cake and decorate with coffee beans, shaved chocolate or wild strawberries.

# CONFITURE DE QUETSCHES D'ALSACE AUX NOIX ET A LA CANNELLE

## *Quetsch Plum and Walnut Jam with Cinnamon*

### MAKES 4-5 5OOG/18OZ JARS
**1kg/2 ¼ lb quetsch or Victoria plums, halved and stoned**
**juice of 1 lemon**
**800g/1 ¾ lb granulated sugar**
**1 cinnamon stick**
**200g/7oz walnuts, roughly chopped**

Put the plums in a preserving pan over a low heat with the lemon juice, sugar and cinnamon until the sugar is dissolved. Bring to the boil, tip into a bowl and leave overnight. Return the fruit to the pan and bring to the boil again. Remove from the heat and skim any scum from the surface with a slotted spoon. Bring back to the boil, remove the cinnamon and stir in the walnuts. Pot up and cover immediately. It will have quite a thin consistency.

FAR RIGHT *Corn cobs festoon an old barn in a farming village of the Sundgau.*
RIGHT *A selection of country breads and Kougelhopfs* from Sundgau baker Monsieur Ruf *(see page 83).*
BELOW *A typical landscape in the Jura Alsacien right on the Swiss border, with the village of Kiffis in the foreground. In the background is Roggenburg which lies in Switzerland.*

# THE SUNDGAU AND THE RHINE PLAIN

The Sundgau – whose name means simply 'southern county' – is a special corner of Alsace. In the days of Charlemagne, Alsace was a duchy of the Holy Roman Empire, divided into the Nordgau and the Sundgau. After the Revolution, when France's *départements* were set up, the 'northern county' became the Bas-Rhin and the 'southern county' the Haut-Rhin. Though the old terms no longer have any official meaning, the Sundgau is very much alive in spirit, and the name is familiar to all *alsaciens* even if the precise limits of the territory are rather vague. Broadly speaking, today it includes the area south of Mulhouse as far as the first folds of the Jura range which forms the border with Switzerland.

This is rolling agricultural country, a land flowing with milk and honey (though full-time farmers and bee-keepers are a dying breed here), home of sundry healers, water diviners – and commuters to Switzerland. Distant views of both Vosges and Jura frame the landscape. Majestic mixed broadleaf and evergreen forests alternate with grazing pastures and orchards. Fish ponds punctuate the countryside, and streams and rivers divide up the area into a series of valleys. Storks nest on church roofs, herons stand pensively on one leg in the fields, buzzards circle idly around.

Past temporal rulers of the Sundgau have included the antecedents of St Odile (patron saint of Alsace), the counts of Ferrette and the Habsburgs, while for its spiritual direction this southern province has looked to the bishoprics of both Strasbourg and of Basle. At the conclusion of the Thirty Years War, under the terms of the Treaty of Westphalia, the Habsburgs were shown the door, the counts of Ferrette once more became landlords and the Sundgau was gradually repopulated – largely by the Swiss. The peaceful eighteenth century saw a development in agriculture and the establishment of several important Jewish settlements as immigrants arrived from Germany, Hungary and Poland. In Mulhouse the textile industry was born, which was to make the city 'the Manchester of France'.

Though its proximity to Switzerland and the purchasing power of the Swiss franc have undoubtedly influenced the character of the place today, the Sundgau remains a charming, rural backwater. It is a delightful region in which to walk, bicycle or take a horse-drawn buggy, the slow pace enabling one to admire the timber-framed multi-coloured houses which are steadily being restored to their former glory. At regular intervals along the way, *carpes frites* (see page 80) are offered, the Sundgau's greatest gastronomic claim to fame. (To those who would mock, it should be pointed out that the *Routes de la Carpe Frite* were

*TOP Jean-Marie Heine of the Bouton d'Or cheese shop with a splendid tray of Munsters. Munster is thought to have been pioneered originally by the Irish monks who settled the Vosges in the ninth century. It is a soft cheese with a slightly orange brine-washed crust, a peculiarly powerful smell and a rich creamy taste. Its colour is attributable to a particular bacterium,* Bacterium linens, *which is naturally present in the cellar where the cheeses are ripened. After the initial attack of Munster's penetrating aroma, its smooth taste comes as something of an agreeable surprise.*
*ABOVE Goats' cheeses and Langres tastefully arranged on typical Alsace pottery.*

recently nominated a *Site Remarquable du Goût* by the Conseil National des Arts Culinaires, an event which caused a swelling of pride in Sundgau hearts and much jubilation amongst local producers, hoteliers and restaurateurs.)

# MULHOUSE

The city's name (pronounced 'mew-looz') and symbol (a mill wheel) evoke a time when it was set about with numerous watermills; it was then a magnificent and prosperous textile centre. After many years in the doldrums it is now enjoying something of a renaissance; the centre has recently been put down to cobbles and banned to traffic. Famous for its museums (veteran cars and trains on the outskirts, textiles and the charming Musée Historique in the centre) and for its high immigrant population, Mulhouse is not, in fairness, a place to put at the top of one's Alsace itinerary; it is, however, many people's point of entry into the region as it shares an airport with Basle.

The city's Saturday market is a vivid and accurate reflection of the ethnic mix to be found in Mulhouse today. Inside the covered hall and out on the forecourt, farmers' wives from the Vosges, selling Munster cheese and free-range eggs, rub shoulders amiably enough with north Africans whose stands are piled high with several varieties of mint, fresh coriander, multi-coloured peppers and exotic fruits. Though an age-old institution, the character of the market has changed over the years with the influx of immigrants. '*Aujourd'hui le marché est coloré différemment*' remarks one stallholder ('nowadays the market has a different colour'). But another jokes, '*Nous, on regarde les sous, on ne regarde pas la couleur!*' ('It's the colour of people's money which matters, not the colour of their skin!').

The place de la Réunion in the centre is the scene each spring and autumn of an open-air textile market. Gorgeous bolts of richly coloured furnishing fabrics festoon the trestle tables, recalling briefly Mulhouse's glorious history as textile manufacturer for the salons of Paris (and the White House). The tall buttercup yellow house in one corner of the square is the famous Bouton d'Or, purveyor of fine cheeses to a widely scattered, cheese-loving clientele. Jacques, the town's most celebrated *pâtissier*, is next door, while on the other side of the square is a branch of CCA (La Charcuterie Alsacienne), an excellent *boucherie-charcuterie* with shops all over the region. The interiors are attractively panelled in light wood decorated with traditional floral motifs. Alsace has some of the finest and most varied *charcuterie* in all of France; they make a wonderful gift, and CCA provides at small cost, for just such a purpose, a stout cardboard gift box like a hinged coffer, decorated like the shop's painted wood panelling.

One of the best shopping streets is the rue du Sauvage. (When, in the dark days of the annexation of Alsace, all streets were re-named in German, the rue du Sauvage became – to the delight of locals – Adolf Hitler-Strasse. The German commandant was apparently unaware of any unfortunate connotations.) Here are to be found Les Petites Halles, selling exotic fruit, vegetables, herbs, bread and cheese, and a great coffee shop (Au Bon Nègre) from which issues forth an irresistible aroma of freshly roasted beans.

*LEFT The* tricolore *flutters proudly outside the colourful and imposing Hôtel de Ville on the place de la Réunion in Mulhouse. The city, staunchly Protestant and more Swiss than French in character, was for a long time an independent republic. On 15 March 1798 the city proclaimed its adherence to France, laid down its arms, lowered the local flag and hoisted the* tricolore *in its place.*
*TOP A beautifully restored house on the corner of the main square, next door to the famous Pâtisserie Jacques.*
*ABOVE Assorted pastries at the Pâtisserie Jacques, including croissants, Streussels (with the crumble topping),* pains au chocolat, *savarins, brioches and apple turnovers.*

## CARPES FRITES

*A glimpse at the map of the Sundgau shows a huge concentration of small ponds, which are caused by an immense underground reservoir of natural springs. In these calm, untroubled waters laze fat carp. No one seems to know why or when carp became a feature of the Sundgau. Perhaps the Jewish settlers who arrived in large numbers in the eighteenth century (they were permitted to work in Switzerland but obliged to return to the Sundgau at sundown) brought with them not only a taste for the fish but also expertise in both the raising and the cooking of it. Whatever the reason, carp is firmly anchored in the gastronomy of the area. The fish is customarily cut in sections across the bone or (more rarely) filleted. 'Carpes frites sans arêtes' means 'carp without bones', rather than 'non-stop fried carp' – though, given the quantity in which they are served and the steady pace at which they keep coming to the table, the latter translation might seem to be the correct one. The sections are dusted in soft wheat semolina (semoule de blé tendre) to give a breadcrumb-like effect, and either pan-fried or deep-fried. The fish is served with either chips or lemon wedges and a green salad.*

*TOP A lovely old pack bridge leads to the Chapelle St Brice near Hausgauen. CENTRE LEFT At the Ferme-Auberge Paradisvogel in Bernwiller the family serves simple plats du jour and bakes its own bread. CENTRE RIGHT The Rhone-Rhine canal flows through the Sundgau, linking these two great rivers. LEFT Many farms in the Sundgau sell their own home-reared produce on the premises. OPPOSITE TOP AND BOTTOM Local charcuterie.*

Around Christmas time, Mulhouse bakers make a special St Nicholas bread called *Schnackla*. These are to the city as *Männala* (see page 26) are to other parts of Alsace. Made from the same lightly sweetened and enriched dough, *Schnackla* (meaning 'little snail' in dialect) have a snail-like shape a bit like a reversed letter 's'. For the best *bretzels*, locals go to Roland on the rue des Puits, behind the dramatic, newly built arts centre La Filature, or to Au Bretzel Chaud on the rue du Sauvage. And for the widest choice of beers (which go together with *bretzels* as steak with kidney), the somewhat teutonic Brasserie Gambrinus on the rue des Franciscains – which stocks thirty draught and more than a thousand bottled beers – is the place to go.

A spirit of competition is apparently not the main motivation of the various Winstub-type venues in the centre: all offer an identical choice of typical Alsatian dishes (*Fleischschnacka, Lawerknapfla, choucroute* and *tarte a l'oignon*) though Le Petit Zinc stands out from the crowd with its bistro-style atmosphere and decor. The lovely art deco Hotel du Parc has a restaurant and lively bar, while in the suburb of Riedesheim there are two fine restaurants, La Poste and La Tonnelle.

South-west of Mulhouse, the monastery of Notre Dame d'Oelenberg near Reiningue is worth a visit, whether for spiritual or bodily refreshment. In the community shop the Trappist monks sell their cheese, produce from the kitchen garden, honey from the hives, coarsely ground flour from their mill and some particularly well-flavoured home-made noodles.

True to its *paysan* image (though it should be noted that *paysan* does not mean peasant, but farmer), the Sundgau has a number of lively agricultural markets. Bernwiller's *Altbürafascht* (old-time farmers' festival) held in September is the best, a real celebration of the village's original farming character. Corn is harvested and threshed *à l'ancienne*, Bulldog tractors from the Fifties converge on the village, a cortège of *paysans* decked out in their colourful Sundgau costumes parades through the streets, mountains of *choucroute* are consumed and the band plays on. The inhabitants of the village have for some reason always been known as *Paradiesvogel* (birds of paradise). The name has been adopted by the *ferme-auberge* on the main street, which serves regional dishes, home-made pasta, and bread straight from the wood-fired oven.

## ALTKIRCH AND LES TROIS VALLEES

Altkirch is the capital of the Sundgau – though 'capital' seems a grand word for this small, sleepy town set high up on a hill within its ramparts. Once a year, in November, the Marché Ste Catherine takes over the whole town. Formerly a major cattle and agricultural market for the whole area (and by tradition also a 'marriage market', Ste Catherine being the patron saint of spinsters), the goods on sale nowadays are neither particularly local nor especially agricultural. But Ste Catherine's legacy lives on in the tradition of 'Les Catherinettes' which is celebrated around this time. Unattached young women of twenty-five years old, apparently unabashed at indicating their single status, spend the day sporting spectacular hats designed and made by friends and family.

South of Altkirch are three gentle valleys – de la Largue, de l'Ill and du Thalbach – each named after the river or stream which wanders slowly through it. The Largue valley is *carpe frite* country, and fish ponds abound. In the village of Hindlingen, with about four hundred inhabitants, there are upwards of sixty ponds, some of them in private hands, others owned by professional carp farmers.

Some of the Sundgau's best *carpes frites* (see page 80) are to be found at the Restaurant Le Soleil (also known as chez Wadel) in neighbouring Ueberstrass. It would be hard to find a warmer welcome or wider smile than Madame Wadel's. The ample (and equally beaming) Monsieur Wadel dusts the cross-sections of fish in semolina in the time-honoured tradition, fries them crisp and perfectly dry and sends them forth with a mountain of *pommes frites*, lemon wedges and a crunchy green salad with finely chopped onion. The watery landscape of the Largue valley is also suited to snails, which Monsieur Gissinger (a member of Sundgau Terroir) raises in his *escargotières* in Hindlingen. These he turns into *choux aux escargots* (snail puffs with garlic butter), snail quiches and other gasteropodous delicacies, to the delight of his customers.

The Ill valley runs gently down through the villages of Grentzingen and Oberdorf, which have some of the best *maisons à colombages* (half-timbered houses) in the neighbourhood. Arranged in an almost unbroken line along the main street, they are all set sideways on to the road; every window is bursting with geraniums, courtyards are neatly swept and little front gardens immaculately kept. Many of the geraniums will have been bought at the lively street market held in May in Durmenach, when the whole village is given over to stands selling bedding plants, sundry sausagery, garden and farm implements and seasonal fruit and vegetables. Corks pop, draught beer is liberally dispensed and the air is filled with smells of *tartes flambées* and barbecued sausages. Feldbach is the most southerly village on the recently created *Route Romane*. Its twelfth-century Romanesque church was sensitively restored in the Sixties to a state of simple, quiet beauty by an association of friends.

Oltingue's Musée Paysan is housed in a typical *maison sundgauvienne*, with artefacts and costumes from the immediate area, as well as an old kitchen and scullery. An antique *Baeckeoffe* dish, fitted with an iron band and a padlock, is one of the items on display. In the old days families would take the dish to the baker's to be cooked (see recipe, page 100). The band was designed to ensure that others (whose *Baeckeoffe* might be less well endowed) could not pinch any of the contents for their own pot. The village has a most original gîte: like a tiny Hansel and Gretel house, painted in a vivid shade of blue, it stands on the main street. The Ill tumbles through the village of Lutter, past the Hostellerie Paysanne, one of the best places to stay in the Sundgau. Serving as the annexe of the Auberge Paysanne (see recipes page 94), this fine half-timbered building was saved from extinction by the lively *patronne* Madame Litzler and reconstructed on its present site.

The third valley, the Thalbach, is especially appealing in the spring when the cherry trees are in blossom. Obermorschwiller has some fine old dwellings, some with a bread oven resembling a mini-house on stilts attached to the side of the building, complete with its own 'beavers-tail' tiled roof. The exterior wall of the oven is of wattle and daub, often roughcast in the same colour as the house. The inside is lined with fire bricks. The oven is accessible

*OPPOSITE TOP A* boulangerie *on wheels brings fresh bread to the villages.*
*OPPOSITE CENTRE Mellow, half-timbered houses in Grentzingen.*
*OPPOSITE BOTTOM A neatly tended cottage garden in Grentzingen.*
*RIGHT A geranium-decked window of a house in Illhauesern.*
*BELOW Weeping willows bend low to the river Ill as it flows gently past the gardens of the celebrated three-star Auberge de l'Ill. On the right is the Maison du Pêcheur, the honeymoon suite of the Hotel des Berges.*

## MONSIEUR RUF'S PAINS AU FEU DE BOIS

*Monsieur Ruf was not always a baker. His first profession was building and repairing the fine old tiled stoves and bread ovens of the Sundgau. He started baking on a modest level with a few loaves ('pour le plaisir') using old family recipes. Nowadays he makes pain paysan, sourdough (pain au levain), and six or seven other different sorts. Work starts at midnight, when the doughs are mixed one by one, gently kneaded and then left to rise. Flours (wholewheat, rye, spelt and unbleached) are acquired partly locally, partly from the Kircher mill in Ebersheim near Sélestat which specializes in stoneground flours. Added interest and fibre comes from sunflower seeds, linseeds, oatmeal and, walnuts. The ovens have one piece of electronic gadgetry, a slightly melted plastic digital timer hanging above the door. For the rest, they are entirely wood-fired using a mixture of ash, hazel, birch and hornbeam, all of it felled and cut to size by the Ruf family. By midday the breads are baked and Monsieur Ruf is ready for a nap. In the afternoon he sets off in his bread van to sell his wares.*

## BERNARD ANTONY, THE BIG CHEESE IN THE SUNDGAU

*Hidden away in the deepest recesses of the Jura Alsacien, in the village of Vieux-Ferrette, is the* Sundgauer Käskeller. *Its owner, Bernard Antony, is an arch crusader in the cause for raw milk farmhouse cheeses.*
*A* Maître Fromager *and member of the* Ordre des Fromagers de la Confrérie de St Uguzon, *he takes such joy in his product that his face lights up when he speaks and his voice is full of missionary fervour for the cheeses which – due to the combined efforts of Brussels, the giant food processing groups and the* grandes surfaces *(supermarkets) – he fears may one day disappear. He corresponds periodically with the Prince of Wales, whom he perceives to be a fellow believer in the cause, and seldom misses an opportunity to defend and promote his beloved* fromages au lait cru. *Monsieur Antony is an* affineur: *he receives young cheeses from selected sources all over France (and some from England), ripens them to the correct degree of perfection and sells them at the* Käskeller *or from his magnificent cheese-mobile at various markets in the Sundgau. Cheese feasts are staged at the* Käskeller *by special request.*

from the kitchen via a little hinged iron door through which the furnace is fed with wood, the embers are raked free and the bread is put in for baking. At the tail end of the valley is Michelbach- (pronounced locally as in 'stickleback') le-Haut, a village with a strong bread-making tradition which stages a lively Fête du Pain on the second Sunday in September each year. It is also the home of Monsieur Ruf and his wonderful country breads (see page 83). At La Marmite, in nearby Muespach *chef-patron* Jean-Luc Wahl makes a speciality of fish dishes, many of them locally inspired.

## THE JURA ALSACIEN

The southernmost part of the Sundgau, which sits snugly up against the Swiss border, is known as the Jura Alsacien. The dramatic ruins of the castle of Ferrette and the well-preserved *vieille ville* cling precariously to the steep hillside above the town centre. Neighbouring Vieux-Ferrette is the base of an enterprising organization known as Sundgau Terroir, which groups together a number of local producers keen to diversify outside their traditional farming activities and to establish links directly with the consumer. This they can do at the small markets in Altkirch and Waldighoffen, in their shop in Ferrette and on the farm. There is a wonderfully eclectic range of locally grown produce from which to choose: sundry seasonal vegetables, asparagus, soft fruits, goats' cheese, honey, free-range poultry and eggs, snail delicacies, *pain paysan*, dairy products, flowers and plants.

Georges and Liliane Baudroux at the Auberge du Vieux Moulin de Bendorf are also members of Sundgau Terroir. Their specialities include home-made foie gras, terrines, sausages and goats' cheese; in their restaurant they serve roast kid, guinea fowl and turkey, and country bread from the artisanal bakery in the village. A number of hostelries in the Jura Alsacien cater for the large number of walkers and cyclists who frequent the area. The Auberge du Morimont, built in the seventeenth century, does a brisk trade at the weekends and serves a range of local dishes, many to be ordered in advance. At the foot of the Jura hills, with unrivalled views into Switzerland from the terrace, is the Hotel-Restaurant Petit Kohlberg where the welcome is warm, the food robust and uncomplicated and plenty of the raw materials come from the home farm.

Tucked away down a forest track near Oltingue is the tiny Auberge St Brice, named after the little chapel dedicated to the saint of that name. On summer evenings the courtyard and benches set out on the grass under a huge chestnut tree are alive with the buzz of happy visitors tucking into hunks of *Kougelhopf au lard* (bacon and walnut Kougelhopf) with one of the best Munster cheeses to be found locally. Other specialities (made to order) include *tarte à l'oignon, Baeckeoffe* and *coq au Riesling.* Max the donkey observes proceedings from his hut, his familiar bray working up to a crescendo as the arrival of Michel (tenant of the Auberge and linchpin of the bank in Oltingue) reminds him that it's time for his supper too.

The village of Lucelle is well known to bibliophiles with culinary leanings for its connections with Bernard Buchinger, Abbott of Lucelle and author of the famous *Kochbuch*, published in Molsheim in 1671. Designed for the use of both religious and lay households

ABOVE *Wild flowers flourish in the meadows of the Sundgau (here deep in the Jura Alsacien), untouched by the plough, fertilized only by cow pats and mown mainly by munching brown and white cows. It is a walkers' paradise where the right to roam is freely granted and greatly enjoyed by walkers at all levels, often equipped with a picnic containing many local delicacies.*
RIGHT *A typical Sundgau bread oven, attached to the outside of the house and set on*

*a platform or sometimes on stilts. Access to the oven is through a little cast iron door in the kitchen, through which wood is fed for the fire. Once the oven is hot, the embers are raked out or aside and the bread baked directly on the floor of the oven, hence its often ash-dusted underside. Most often bread will be a variant of* pain paysan *made with a mixture of rye and wheat flours.*
OPPOSITE *Two beautiful old houses adorned with flowers in the town of Buschwiller.*

of the time, the *Kochbuch* constitutes a fascinating piece of social and culinary history (a copy can be seen in the University Library of Strasbourg). Little remains of the once vast and powerful Cistercian abbey, but a model in the tiny 'museum' gives some idea of the scope of the building and the influence of the community before the Revolution.

From Lucelle the road (known as the Internationale Strasse, and out of bounds to soldiers in uniform, a relic of the days when these border roads were highly sensitive areas) skirts the Swiss-French border beside the River Lucelle before heading up into the hills to Kiffis. The beautiful blue-and-yellow timbered farmhouses on the edge of this tiny village belong to the Walther family (see Le Cheval Blanc, page 92). Horses can be hired for a ride along the bridle-paths through the wonderful countryside and forests surrounding the village.

Though by nature an agricultural area, the Sundgau has never had a cheese-making tradition. Recently some small-scale goats' cheese production has been getting under way: Monsieur Fernex (another member of Sundgau Terroir) in Biederthal and the Wyss-Christen family in Leymen sell goats' cheeses from the farm, and at local markets in both Switzerland and France. The big cheese event of the area is held at the end of August each year in Hagenthal – the spectacular Salon du Vin et Fromage – to which producers of wine and cheese (and other gustatory pleasures) flock from all over France to sell their wares to an eager audience from the Basle area and neighbouring Markgräflerland in Germany.

The hotel-restaurant Jenny, between Hagenthal and Hégenheim, is another favourite watering hole of Baslers (the border is visible from the dining room). The brasserie serves a selection of typical dishes, including (for Saturday lunch) a classic *pot-au-feu à l'alsacienne*, a dish of boiled beef served, unlike in other parts of France, with an array of salads – radish, celeriac, tomatoes, cucumber, carrots and beetroot – and the indispensable, sinus-blasting snort of horseradish sauce. Down the road in Buschwiller the old school house has been transformed into the Restaurant La Couronne. Philippe and Elizabeth Lacour – he from the Vosges, she from Bournemouth – met when working together in the Dordogne. The food is a happy amalgam of Alsace, Périgord and England: a *confit de canard* is served with *choucroute*, miniature *tartes flambées* are garnished with snails and smoked salmon (see page 96), and home-made sorbets come cradled in a brandysnap basket.

Best for fine wines in the Sundgau is the banal-looking supermarket in Hegenheim, owned by the eponymous Monsieur Freund, who will raise his hat and uncork a bottle of some priceless nectar to share with you, in the certain knowledge that you will find it impossible to go away without buying a case. Round the corner at the Caves des Frères Grèder, Edgar Luttringer is an engaging and genial guide to the wines of the Eguisheim co-operative (Wolfberger) and other *bonnes bouteilles*. The Moulin Jenny in Hésingue, a flour mill dating back to 1379 and still active, was once owned by the powerful abbots of Murbach (see page 111). Much of the semolina used locally to coat *carpes frites* comes from the Moulin, while the wholewheat and baking flours milled here are sold to bakeries and private customers throughout the area.

Blessed by the fertile alluvial soils of the Rhine basin, Huningue and Village Neuf are famous for their market gardens whose speciality in springtime is asparagus. Local people, and the Swiss and German gastrotourists who come in great numbers on asparagus

pilgrimages, favour the white sort, for which the asparagus is trenched (grown entirely below ground) and thereby blanched. Top chefs increasingly prefer their asparagus green (grown above ground), or mauve-tipped (trenched but allowed just to put its nose above the soil, at which point it takes on a little colour). Some restaurants, such as Biry in Village Neuf, are open only during the season, and serve only asparagus with ham and the regulation three sauces: hollandaise, mayonnaise and vinaigrette.

## THE RHINE PLAIN

Leaving behind the Sundgau, the flat and immensely fertile plain of the Rhine and the Ill presents yet another unique landscape. The southern part, the Hardt, is fast turning into a vast maize and wheat plantation, relentlessly irrigated by bird-like sprinklers with a wingspan the width of a football pitch. Further north is the Ried, where the richly fertile earth is dark brown like bitter chocolate, and the magnificent farmhouses in villages such as Ohnenheim are evidence of the importance of agriculture over many centuries.

Game is plentiful in the plain: families of wild boar can occasionally be spotted trotting purposefully across the fields in single file, and roe deer lie low in the copses and woods. The rivers – if one is expecting a scenic drive along the banks – are sadly inaccessible: the Rhine proper (known as '*le vieux Rhin*', the old Rhine) is hidden away on the other side of the canal with which it runs parallel most of the way from Basle to Strasbourg. The Ill is most in evidence when it bursts its banks, which happens several times a year.

But this one-time haven for smallholders, game, migratory birds and solitary fishermen is under great threat from twentieth-century 'progress'. After the Second World War the river became an industrial dustbin and fishing ceased to be a practical or economic proposition. For a time the only vestiges of this once important activity were to be found in the Ecomusée in the fisherman's cottage from Artolsheim, which houses a permanent exhibition devoted to the lifestyle and habits of a fishing family of the Ried. Much of the fertile land along the river fell prey to agri-business, the flood pastures were drained, ploughed up and cultivated. The Rhine plain seemed threatened, and the river a shadow of its former, bountiful self.

Recently, however, thanks to the initiative of an active group of conservationists who were alarmed by the way in which the landscape was being inexorably changed, the Rhine plain is slowly regaining some of its original character. Once again fish are caught in both rivers – and even the salmon are back. A delicate cheese called Tomme des Prés du Ried is made in Muttersholtz from the milk of cows which graze on the watery pastures beside the Ill. Close by, the Kircher mill in Ebersheim near Sélestat, another endeavour devoted to keeping alive old products and traditional ways of doing things, sells a good range of stone-ground flours of various sorts. These are small beginnings and tiny enterprises but they signal hope for the unique landscape and lifestyle of the Rhine plain.

BOTTOM *Monsieur and Madame Vonarb*
*smoke and cook certain fish to order,*
*including eel and crayfish.*
BELOW Tourtes *in Alsace are generally made of*
*pork and veal. The Vonarbs make a*
*delicious variation on the theme using Rhine fish*
*bound together in a savoury* mousseline
*and baked in puff pastry. The pies are made*
*fresh to order and sold locally to private clients*
*or in small supermarkets in nearby villages.*

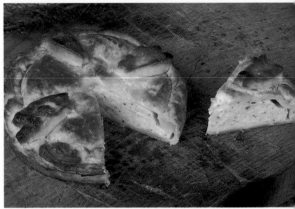

## ADRIEN VONARB, PROFESSIONAL RHINE FISHERMAN

*Monsieur Vonarb – like the Rhine salmon – is a member of a species which had all but disappeared*
*and is now, once more, making a comeback. A keen amateur angler, he decided in 1988*
*to try and make a living from what had previously been a hobby. Nets were purchased, tanks were*
*built for short-term storage of fish (much of which is sold live, or killed only when an*
*order is received), and a kitchen was equipped for converting part of the catch into marketable*
*products. On a good day his nets, which are placed at intervals along the old Rhine*
*and on the parallel canal, may yield* sandre *(zander),* brochet *(pike),* anguille *(eel),* écrevisses *(cray-*
*fish),* lotte de rivière *(burbot),* brème *(bream) and tiny fish for* friture; *on a bad day, when*
*the snows upstream are melting and the icy water thunders down, the fish wisely lie low and the nets*
*are loaded only with leaves and debris ('que des feuilles Suisses!' he snorts –*
*'nothing but Swiss leaves!'). For Monsieur Vonarb there is no such distinction as 'noble fish' and*
*'common fish' – everything has its use. Some fish is sold fresh to private customers*
*and top chefs throughout the region; eel, trout and carp are smoked to order; and the Vonarbs also*
*make a range of delicious* tourtes, terrines *and* quiches *which are sold at various*
*outlets in the surrounding area.*

# L'ANCIENNE FORGE

**68220 HAGENTHAL-LE-HAUT, Tel 89 68 56 10**

*Until the 1970s the Ancienne Forge was the workshop of the village smithy. In 1985 the small, half-timbered house just off the main street was rescued from ruin and converted into a restaurant by Monsieur and Madame Baumann. The roughcast walls were painted a warm salmon pink, the windows were festooned with geraniums and petunias, and chef Hervé Paulus was hired. He describes his food as 'une cuisine du terroir créative, avec un petit bout du soleil' ('local, creative cooking dappled with sunlight'), for which the restaurant recently received its first* macaron *(Michelin star). The wine list is short but well chosen: Alsace wines from Kaysersberg and Eguisheim, and bottles from Bordeaux, Burgundy and the Rhone.*

## LA CHARLOTTE AUX POINTES D'ASPERGES A LA MOUSSE DE JAMBON

### Ham Mousses with Asparagus Tips

*Hervé Paulus plays on a traditional Alsace theme – asparagus with ham – in these creamy ham mousses braced by spears of green and white asparagus. Fine-stalked sprue asparagus is ideal for this dish as the stalks should be no thicker than your little finger or you will not have sufficient tips to line the moulds. The stems are blended with cream and sherry to make a sauce. (Illustrated opposite, left)*

**SERVES 6**
**1kg/2¼ lb white asparagus, peeled**
**1kg/2¼ lb green asparagus, trimmed**
**2tsp sugar**
**3 sheets gelatine or 1½ tsp powdered gelatine**
**600ml/21fl oz whipping cream**
**300g/10 oz cooked ham**
**100g/3½ oz smoked raw ham, finely diced**
**2tbsp dry sherry**
**salt and freshly ground black pepper**

Cut the top 8cm/3in from the asparagus spears. Bring 2 saucepans of salted water to the boil and add 1 teaspoon of sugar to each. Cook the tips in one saucepan for 8-10 minutes or until barely tender. Drain the tips, refresh in cold water and cut them into 4cm/1½ in long pieces. Cook the stems in the other saucepan for about 15 minutes or until quite soft. Line a tray or baking sheet with cling film and place on it 6 aluminium rings 8cm/3in in diameter and 4cm/1½ in high. (You can improvise by using 200g/7oz tuna cans with tops and bottoms removed.) Arrange the asparagus tips upright around the inside of the rings, alternating the colours.

Soak the sheets of gelatine in cold water until floppy. Squeeze them out and put them in a small saucepan with 3 tablespoons of the cream. Heat gently to dissolve. If using powdered gelatine, soak it in 3 tablespoons of water until spongy, then dissolve it over a gentle heat. Put the cooked ham in a food processor or liquidizer and process finely. With the motor running, add the dissolved gelatine and cream/water mixture through the funnel. Beat 500ml/16fl oz of the cream into soft peaks and fold it into the ham purée, along with the raw ham cubes. Spoon the

mixture into the asparagus-lined rings, smooth the tops with the back of a wetted teaspoon and refrigerate for several hours.

Blend the green and white asparagus stems separately in the liquidizer, adding half of the remaining cream to each colour. Push the purées through a sieve to eliminate the threads, season to taste and add 1 tablespoon of sherry to each.

To serve the mousses, pour a little pool of both sauces side by side onto each plate. Lift the mousses with a spatula and place them over the sauces. Remove the rings.

# TOURNEDOS DE LOTTE LARDE A LA COMPOTE D'OIGNONS AU ROUGE D'ALSACE

### 'Tournedos' of Monkfish with a Compote of Spring Onions and Red Wine

*For this delicious entrée, chef Hervé Paulus surrounds the medallions of monkfish with thin rashers of streaky bacon. The pig caul is*
*optional, but it does help to keep the 'tourne-dos' together as they are fried. The compote of spring onions is made by gently stewing them in the best part of a bottle of Pinot Noir from Alsace. (Illustrated above, right)*

**SERVES 4**
**1 monkfish tail weighing about 1kg/2¼ lb**
**1 carrot**
**1 onion**
**1 bouquet garni**
**4 slices smoked streaky bacon, rinds removed**
**a piece of pig caul, optional**
**a little olive oil**
**900g/2lb spring onions (scallions), finely sliced**
**200g/7oz unsalted butter**
**1 bottle rouge d'Alsace (Pinot Noir)**
**salt and freshly ground black pepper**

Skin the monkfish and cut the two fillets from either side of the backbone. Chop up the bone and put in a large saucepan with the carrot, onion and bouquet garni, cover with water and simmer gently for 30 minutes. Strain the stock, return it to the saucepan and reduce it to about half a cupful by fast boiling.

Cut each fillet into thick slices and season. Put 2 or 3 slices together side by side to make four 'tournedos' of fish, each weighing about 125g/4½oz. Wrap the bacon around the 'tournedos' to brace them and secure with toothpicks or wrap in caul. Brush with olive oil and set aside on a plate in the refrigerator.

To make the onion compote, heat 50g/2oz of the butter in a saucepan and soften the spring onions in it without allowing them to take colour – about 10 minutes. Season with salt and pepper to taste. Add two-thirds of the bottle of wine and cook briskly until the wine is almost evaporated and the onions are nicely syrupy. Put the remaining wine in a saucepan and reduce to about half a cupful. Add the reduced fish stock.

Heat some more olive oil in a non-stick saucepan and cook the 'tournedos' for 6-8 minutes until lightly coloured and just done, turning them once.

Whisk the remaining butter into the red wine and stock reduction. Check the seasoning.

Arrange some onion compote in the centre of each plate, put a 'tournedo' on top of the compote and surround it with some of the red wine and butter sauce.

## LE CHEVAL BLANC

**68480 KIFFIS, Tel 89 40 33 05**

The Cheval Blanc is owned and run by various members of the Walther clan: André is in the kitchen, Agnès runs the dining room with the help of André's wife; Francis is behind the bar and attends to the bills. Madame Walther mère is in the background, ironing tablecloths or taking care of a fractious grandchild. Almost all of the vegetables and salads come from the kitchen garden behind the restaurant, supplemented on occasion with dandelions and puff-balls picked fresh from the fields and wild garlic culled from the woods. All André's cooking is done on a venerable old wood-fired stove, and many of the recipes for traditional Sundgau dishes (for which the restaurant is justly famous) come from André's grandmother. 'I'm a bit of a conservative really', he admits, 'I like to do things the old way'. His Baeckeoffe (see page 100), a combination of lamb, pork, beef and vegetables, lavishly spiced and gently baked for hours, is an explosion of flavours, and his carpes frites come recommended by Maître Antony (see page 84), the cheesemonger in Ferrette who has been known to make and break many a local reputation.

## CARPES FRITES DU SUNDGAU

### Fried Carp

Sections or darnes of carp are dusted in fine semolina and pan-fried until they are crisp and crusty. This Sundgau classic is served with lemon wedges, green salad and (sometimes) pommes frites to gild the lily – though André prefers the more simple accompaniment of plainly boiled potatoes straight from his garden. (Illustrated opposite)

**FOR 6**
**2 large carp (about 1.5kg/3½ lb each)**
**fine semolina for coating**

300g/10oz plain flour, sifted
1 pkt (11g/1tbsp) baking powder
pinch of salt

**FOR THE SAUCE**
200g/7oz each of raspberries, redcurrants
and wild cranberries
sugar, to taste
whipped cream to serve

Preheat the oven to 180°C/350°F/gas mark 4. Grease and flour a long loaf tin 40 x 12cm/16 x 5in by 8cm/3in deep. Beat together the egg yolks with half the sugar and the vanilla until light and well creamed. Beat in the wine and oil. Fold in the flour and baking powder. Beat the egg whites with the salt until they form soft peaks. Sprinkle on the remaining sugar, beat until stiff, and then fold into the mixture. Tip into the tin and bake for 40-45 minutes or until a skewer stuck in the middle comes out clean.

Process or blend together the fruit with sugar to taste. Serve the cake with the sauce and a bowl of whipped cream.

2tbsp oil
25g/1oz unsalted butter
salt
lemon wedges, to garnish

Scale, clean and behead the carp (or have the fishmonger or angler do this for you). Cut the body of the fish in 1cm/½in cross-cut slices, right across the bones. Wash the slices well and pat dry on paper towels. Season the fish slices with salt, but not pepper, and roll them in semolina, shaking off any excess.

Heat the oil and butter in a heavy-based frying pan. Fry the fish over a moderate heat for 5-6 minutes, then turn it and cook the other side. You might have to do this in batches. Drain on paper towels and serve at once.

# GATEAU AU VIN BLANC, SAUCE AUX BAIES ROUGES

*Sponge Cake with a Red Berry Sauce*

*(Illustrated right)*

**SERVES 10-12**
4 eggs, separated
300g/10oz caster sugar
a pinch of powdered vanilla or 1tsp
vanilla extract
200ml/7fl oz Edelzwicker or other Alsace
white wine
150ml/5fl oz oil

# BARLAUCHSUPP

## *Wild Garlic Soup*

*Wild garlic, known in dialect as* Bärlauch *(bear garlic), is rampant in the spring in many of the beech forests of the Sundgau. In the old days it was used extensively in popular medicine to aid digestion, to get rid of parasites and to assist the healing of superficial wounds. Nowadays wild garlic is enjoying a culinary renaissance: at the Cheval Blanc (see page 92) it is used in salads.*

SERVES 4
100g/3½oz wild garlic leaves, trimmed and
roughly chopped
100ml/3½fl oz whipping cream
25g/1oz butter
2-3 spring onions or shallots, sliced
2-3 large floury potatoes (about 500g/18oz),
peeled and cubed
salt and freshly ground black pepper

Blanch the wild garlic leaves in 1.1l/2pt of boiling water for 5 minutes. Lift them out with a slotted spoon and reserve the water. Put the leaves and cream in the liquidizer or food processor and reduce to a purée.

Heat the butter in a saucepan and soften the spring onions or shallots gently in it without allowing them to brown. Pour on the reserved cooking water, bring to the boil and toss in the potato cubes. Simmer for 20 minutes, cool a little, then pour into the liquidizer or food processor and blend with the puréed garlic leaves until smooth. Return the soup to the saucepan, bring to the boil and season to taste. Adjust if necessary. Do not allow it to boil for more than a couple of minutes, otherwise the soup will lose its brilliant green colour. Serve at once with good, crusty bread.

# SALADE DE MUNSTER CHAUD

## *Toasted Cheese on a Bed of Salad Leaves*

*Cubes of Munster cheese are set on quarters of sliced bread, put quickly under a fierce grill until bubbly and the toast lightly golden, and set over a salad of mixed leaves in a sherry vinegar dressing. This tasty little starter features on the* menu terroir *in the Auberge Paysanne in Lutter.*

SERVES 4
mixed winter salad leaves such as curly
endive, radicchio, batavia endive
and escarole
1 head of chicory, sliced

FOR THE DRESSING
100ml/3½fl oz oil
4tbsp sherry vinegar
1tsp mustard
pinch of sugar
salt and freshly ground black pepper

5 slices bread, slightly stale, crusts removed
half a Munster cheese, cut into 20 pieces

Arrange the salad leaves decoratively around 4 plates, alternating the colours. Put a bed of chicory in the centre of each plate. To make the dressing, whisk together the oil, vinegar, mustard, sugar, salt and pepper. Drizzle the dressing over the salad leaves.

Preheat the grill to high. Cut the bread slices into quarters. Place one piece of cheese on each quarter slice of bread and grill them until the cheese is melted and the bread lightly toasted. Divide the toasts between the salads and serve immediately.

# SALADE TIEDE AU FLEISCHSCHNACKA

## *Warm Salad with Meat Crêpe Spirals*

*Real* Fleischschnacka *are made by spreading pasta dough with chopped leftover meat (*Fleisch*) – traditionally from a pot-au-feu. The dough is then rolled up in a snail-like spiral (*Schnacka*) and sliced. In this modernized recipe, leftover meat is bound with egg and spread onto crêpes. The crêpes are rolled up, sliced and then fried. (Illustrated opposite)*

SERVES 4
FOR THE HERBY CREPES
125ml/4fl oz milk
100g/3½oz plain flour
2 eggs
1tbsp oil
plenty of fresh chopped herbs such as
chives, chervil, parsley and tarragon
salt and freshly ground pepper

FOR THE FILLING
200g/7oz leftover cooked meat from a roast
or *pot-au-feu*
2 eggs
1-2tbsp whipping cream
2tbsp grated Parmesan, optional
salt and freshly ground pepper

oil for frying
dressed seasonal salad leaves, to serve

To make the crêpe batter, pour 125ml/4fl oz water in a bowl with the milk. Add the flour, eggs, oil and chopped herbs and mix well. Season. Blend to a smooth batter in a food processor or blender. Leave the batter to rest for at least 30 minutes.

Wipe a 20cm/8in frying pan with a lightly oiled paper towel and then heat fiercely. Pour in batter to just cover the bottom of the frying pan. Fry until golden and then turn and fry the other side. The crêpes should be very thin – you should have enough batter to make about 10 crêpes. Set the crêpes aside.

Chop the meat finely in a food processor with the eggs, cream and cheese (if using). Season. Spread the mixture onto 4 crêpes and roll them up. (Interleave the remaining crêpes with freezer paper and freeze for another use.) Slice the filled crêpes diagonally and fry them briskly in hot oil on both sides until golden. Serve over a dressed seasonal salad.

# GALETTES DE MAIS

## *Sweetcorn Pancakes*

*Maize stands tall throughout much of Alsace – though most of it is for cattle rather than human consumption. These gorgeous corny little pancakes are favourites with many top chefs in the area, served with game or with duck. They also go well with the* Cuisses de Poulet à la Bière Ackerland *(see page 43). Once cooked and drained on paper towels, the pancakes can be kept warm in the oven until they are all cooked; if necessary, they can be reheated in a hot oven for a few minutes.*

**MAKES ABOUT 24 PANCAKES**
**2 eggs**
**250ml/8fl oz milk**
**100g/3 ½ oz plain flour**
**300g/10oz tinned sweetcorn, drained**
**salt and freshly ground pepper**
**oil, for frying**

Put all the ingredients in a food processor or liquidizer and process or blend fairly briefly. The flour should be well mixed in, but the corn should retain some character and crunch. Heat a film of oil in a non-stick frying pan and pour in about 1 tablespoon of the batter. Fry the pancake on both sides until golden.

# LE DUO DE TARTES FLAMBEES AU SAUMON ET AUX ESCARGOTS

*Mini* Tartes Flambées *with Salmon and Snails*

*In this variation on the classic* tarte flambée *or* Flammekueche *theme (see page 21), Philippe Lacour of the Restaurant La Couronne in Buschwiller tops the* tartes *with salmon and snails. The dough bases and topping can be prepared in advance and kept chilled ready for baking. There will be more dough than is needed for the recipe: use it for a pizza or make it into a small loaf. (Illustrated above)*

**SERVES 6**
**FOR THE BREAD DOUGH**
**500g/18oz strong white bread flour**
**15g/ ½ oz fresh yeast or 1 pkt easy-blend dry yeast (6g/ ¼ oz )**
**1tsp salt**
**1tsp caster sugar**
**100ml/3 ½ fl oz olive oil**
**about 250ml/8fl oz milk**

**FOR THE *FROMAGE BLANC* TOPPING**
**125g/4 ½ oz full-fat *fromage blanc* (40% fat content)**
**1 egg yolk**
**a splash of Tabasco sauce**
**fresh tarragon or basil, finely chopped**
**salt**

**FOR THE GARNISH**
**250g/9oz skinless, boneless salmon fillet**
**12 tinned snails, medium size**
**15g/ ½ oz butter**
**1 garlic clove, crushed**
**1 shallot, finely chopped**
**salt and freshly ground black pepper**
**olive oil, for sprinkling**
**hazelnut oil, for sprinkling**
**salad leaves, diced tomato, asparagus spears and herbs, to garnish**

Make up the bread dough with the flour, yeast, salt, sugar, olive oil and milk following the instructions on pages 126–7. Encase the bowl in a plastic bag and allow the dough to rise at room temperature for about 2 hours or until doubled in bulk.

Mix together the *fromage blanc*, egg yolk, Tabasco, herbs and salt. Slice the salmon fillet very thinly, season and set aside. Wash the snails thoroughly and cut them in quarters. Heat the butter in a saucepan and soften the garlic and shallot in it. Add the snails to the saucepan and cook for a few minutes.

Preheat the oven to 250°C/475°F/gas mark 9. Knock down the risen dough and cut in half, reserving one half for another use. Roll out very thinly on a floured board and cut out 12 discs 8cm/3in in diameter. Put them on a greased baking sheet.

Spread each disc almost to the edge with the *fromage blanc* mixture. Arrange the salmon slices on half of the discs and the quartered snails on the other half. Bake for 3-4 minutes or until the edges of the dough are lightly golden and the salmon just opaque. Sprinkle the salmon with a little olive oil and the snails with hazelnut oil. Arrange on plates with the chosen garnish and serve at once.

# MATELOTE DE POISSONS DE NOS RIVIERES

*Freshwater Fish Stew with Vegetables and White Wine*

*Madame Vonarb, the fisherman's wife (see page 89), makes her* matelote *with fresh Rhine eels and adds plenty of carrots and leeks for extra flavour and colour, as well as a generous measure of white wine. Here is an adaptation of this stew that combines several different kinds of fish, which can be either freshwater or ocean fish, depending on your preference and on what you have to hand. Serve the stew with fresh pasta, and have lots of crusty bread to hand to mop up the plentiful, creamy juices. (Illustrated opposite)*

SERVES 6 WITH SECOND HELPINGS
about 2kg/4 ½ lb assorted fish on the bone
50g/2oz unsalted butter
1 onion, finely chopped
1 clove garlic, crushed
1 chicken or fish stock cube
1 bouquet garni (with plenty of
parsley stalks)
350g/12oz baby carrots, trimmed (or old
ones, turned into ovals)
350g/12oz leeks, trimmed and cut in
2cm/¾ in lengths
½ bottle dry white wine such as
an Alsace Riesling
250ml/8fl oz crème fraîche
salt and freshly ground black pepper
parsley or chives, to garnish

Remove the heads and tails from the fish, or ask the fishmonger to do this for you, and cut the fish into 2.5cm/1in slices. Melt the butter in a wide deep saucepan (a preserving pan is ideal) and soften the onion and garlic in it. Add 1l/1¾pt of water, the stock cube and bouquet garni. Bring to the boil and add the vegetables. Cook for 8-10 minutes, then taste the vegetables – they should remain a little crunchy. Remove the vegetables with a slotted spoon, cover to keep them warm and set aside. (Leave the bouquet garni in the pan.) Add the wine to the saucepan and simmer for 10 minutes. Season the fish pieces, then add the eel (if using) to the saucepan and simmer for 8-10 minutes. Add the other fish and simmer for 5-6 minutes more or until just opaque. Lift out the fish and put with the vegetables to keep warm. Discard the bouquet garni. Whisk in the crème fraîche and boil hard to reduce and concentrate the sauce. Check the seasoning. Pour the sauce over the fish and vegetables. Sprinkle with parsley or chives and serve in deep bowls.

# MAGRETS DE CANARD
## A LA CHOUCROUTE
## ET AUX POMMES

*Duck Breasts with* Choucroute
*and Apples*

Choucroute *makes an excellent foil for rich
meats like duck.* Galettes de Maïs *(see page 95)
go well with this dish. (Illustrated above)*

**SERVES 6**
25g/1oz unsalted butter
2 shallots, finely chopped
300g/10oz raw *choucroute*
2 tart cooking apples, peeled and diced
3 juniper berries, crushed under a
knife blade
100ml/3 ½ fl oz dry white wine
3-4tbsp crème fraîche
3 duck breasts with skin, weighing about
350g/12oz each

salt and freshly ground black pepper
large piece of pig's caul, for wrapping the
breasts, optional

**FOR THE SAUCE**
small piece of fresh ginger,
sliced, optional
300ml/10fl oz chicken or beef stock
150ml/5fl oz robust red wine
1tbsp red wine vinegar
50g/2oz butter, chilled, to enrich the sauce

*choucroute* stuffing on top of the breasts, bring the skin up and over and score it with a sharp knife. Wrap the duck breasts in caul, if using, and put the breasts skin side uppermost on a cake rack over a roasting pan. Put a little water in the bottom of the pan (to prevent the fat burning and smoking). Roast for 18-20 minutes until the skin is golden and crusty and the meat still slightly pink.

For the sauce, heat the remaining butter in a saucepan and soften the second shallot in it with the ginger (if used). Add the stock and reduce it by half. Add the wine and the vinegar and reduce again by half. Off the heat whisk in the cold butter bit by bit until the sauce is glossy and rich.

# BOUCHEES A LA REINE

## *Vol-au-vents with Diced Chicken, Mushrooms and Sweetbreads*

*In former times this simple, homely dish (known in dialect as* Suppapaschtetler*) was based on the meat from an old boiling fowl. Typically served at huge family get-togethers, it was a mere appetite sharpener before the serious business of* pot-au-feu *or game or other meat dish was embarked upon. Made properly, with the best ingredients and plenty of loving care, it is a wonderful dish.*

**SERVES 6**
**a 1.2kg/2 ¾ lb free-range chicken**
**250ml/8fl oz dry white wine**
**1 onion**
**1 carrot**
**1 stick celery**
**1 leek**
**2-3 cabbage leaves**
**1 bouquet garni**

**400g/14oz sweetbreads (lamb or veal)**
**300g/10oz mushrooms, quartered or sliced**
**75g/3oz unsalted butter**
**juice of ½ lemon**
**50g/2oz plain flour**
**2 egg yolks**
**4tbsp crème fraîche**
**12 pre-cooked vol-au-vents cases,**
**9-10cm/3 ½ -4in diameter**
**salt and freshly ground black pepper**

Put the chicken, wine, onion, carrot, celery, leek, cabbage leaves, bouquet garni, salt and pepper in a saucepan and just cover with water. Bring to the boil then simmer until tender – about 35 minutes. Add the sweetbreads for the last 15 minutes of the cooking time.

Remove the chicken and sweetbreads, and reserve the stock. Discard all the skin and bones from the chicken and cut the meat in bite-sized pieces. Skin the sweetbreads, remove any membrane and break or dice them into pieces. Fry the mushrooms gently in 25g/1oz of the butter with the lemon juice and salt and pepper to taste for 10 minutes until the juices are rendered. Raise the heat and cook hard to evaporate the juices.

Heat the oven to 190°C/375°F/gas mark 5 and put the vol-au-vents in to warm while you make the sauce. Melt the rest of the butter in a large saucepan and stir in the flour. Add 600ml/21fl oz of the reserved stock, stirring vigorously as it comes to the boil. Thin down if necessary with a little more stock. Simmer gently for about 10 minutes. Stir in the sweetbreads, chicken and mushrooms and simmer together briefly. Remove from the heat. Mix together the egg yolks and crème fraîche and stir them into the chicken filling. Spoon some of it into the warm vol-au-vents, serving 2 per person. Keep the rest of the filling warm and serve separately for second helpings.

Heat half of the butter in a saucepan and soften 1 shallot in it. Rinse the *choucroute* thoroughly in cold water, squeeze dry and add to the saucepan together with the apples, juniper berries and wine. Cover and cook gently for 10 minutes. Tip into a bowl and allow to cool. Add the crème fraîche.

Preheat the oven to 220°C/425°F/gas mark 7. Peel and cut away the skin from the duck breasts leaving it attached all along one side. Season the breasts and the skin. Lay the

## POTEE DE HAGENTHAL

### Haricot Beans with Hiriwurscht *Sausages*

*Monsieur Heyer, the butcher in Hagenthal, makes* Hiriwurscht *sausages, typical of the Sundgau. Composed of beef, pork and a special mixture of spices, they are smoked on the premises. When I told him I'd cooked them up with haricot beans for supper, he christened the dish* cassoulet Sundgauvien.

**SERVES 2**
**1tbsp oil**
**1 onion, finely chopped**
**1 garlic clove, crushed**
**400g/14oz tinned peeled plum tomatoes**
**pinch of dried mixed herbs**
**800g/1 ¾ lb tinned haricot (or flageolet)**
**beans, rinsed and drained**
**2 *Hiriwurscht* or other smoked sausage**
**(weighing about 150g/5oz each)**
**salt and freshly ground black pepper**
**sour cream or *fromage blanc*, optional,**
**to garnish**

Heat the oil in a saucepan or small casserole and soften the onion and garlic in it without allowing them to brown. Add the tomatoes and their juice, the herbs and salt and pepper to taste. Cook hard, stirring, until the tomatoes are reduced to quite a thick, well-flavoured sauce. Add the rinsed and drained beans and lay the sausages on top. Lower the heat and cook gently for 10 minutes, just enough to heat through both the beans and the sausages.

Serve in warm soup bowls with a blob of sour cream or *fromage blanc* on top, if wished, and crusty bread on the side to mop up the juices.

## SURLAWERLA

### Diced Liver in a Piquant Sauce

*This recipe is from Madame Jeannine Antony, wife of the cheesemonger in Ferrette. A Sundgau dish par excellence, it often features at the fund-raising lunches frequently held throughout the area by associations as diverse as the* sapeurs-pompiers *(firemen), the blood donors or the footballers. Jeannine uses* foie de génisse *(baby beef liver), but pigs' or calves' liver could be substituted. Typically served with buttered mashed potatoes, the dish also goes well with* Spätzle *(see page 41).*

**SERVES 4**
**1 onion, finely chopped**
**50g/2oz unsalted butter**
**1tbsp oil**
**600g/22oz liver, cut into 1cm/ ½ in strips**
**2tbsp plain flour**
**200-250ml/7-8fl oz stock or water**
**100ml/3 ½ fl oz red wine**
**plenty of chopped parsley**
**1tbsp red wine vinegar**
**salt and freshly ground black pepper**

Heat the butter and oil in a large, heavy frying pan (preferably non-stick) and gently soften the onion in it without allowing it to take colour. Increase the heat, add the liver and toss it on all sides to brown it lightly – not more than 5-6 minutes or it will toughen. Sprinkle on the flour and continue cooking for a few minutes.

Add the stock or water and also the wine, season to taste and bring to the boil, stirring and scraping to dislodge any bits that may have stuck to the pan. Simmer gently for 10 minutes, stirring from time to time. At the last minute stir in the parsley and vinegar.

## BAECKEOFFE DU CHEVAL BLANC

### Oven-baked Lamb, Beef and Pork in White Wine with Vegetables

Baeckeoffe *is a dish of meat layered with potatoes and vegetables, marinated in white wine and baked in a sealed pot for several hours. This version, from the restaurant Cheval Blanc in Kiffis (see page 92) has less meat than most and is richly spiced with cloves, bay leaves and juniper berries. Serve with green salad and plenty of bread to mop up the unthickened juices. (Illustrated opposite)*

**SERVES 6**
**100g/3 ½ oz boneless neck pork**
**100g/3 ½ oz pie veal or use 200g/7oz pork**
**and omit the veal**
**100g/3 ½ oz boneless shoulder of lamb**
**100g/3 ½ oz boneless stewing beef**
**1 pig's foot cut in 4 pieces (optional)**
**sheets of back fat (optional)**
**5 cloves garlic**
**2 carrots, diced**
**2 onions, finely chopped**
**2kg/4 ½ lb firm, waxy potatoes, peeled**
**and sliced**
**1 leek, finely sliced**
**salt and freshly ground black pepper**
**plain flour, to make luting paste**

**FOR THE MARINADE**
**1 clove garlic**
**1tbsp juniper berries**
**6 cloves**
**6 bay leaves**
**2 pinches mixed dried herbs**
**1 carrot, diced**
**1 onion, finely chopped**
**1 bottle dry white wine**

Cut the meat into cubes and put them in a large non-metallic bowl with the pig's foot, garlic, juniper berries, cloves, bay leaves, herbs, carrot, onion and wine. Cover and refrigerate for at least 12 hours and up to 3 days. Strain the meat and vegetables, reserving the marinade. Discard the vegetables. Lightly butter a large, deep casserole with a well-fitting lid. (In Alsace a huge decorated earthenware terrine is traditionally used.) Lay the sheets of back fat (if using) in the bottom. Put half the potatoes on top, season them, then add successive layers of meat and vegetables, seasoning each layer as you go. Finish with a layer of potatoes. Pour on the reserved marinade. It should come about three quarters of the way up the meat and vegetables. If not, add a little water. Make a luting paste with flour and enough water to give the consistency of a wet bread dough. Arrange it over the join between lid and casserole to seal. Bake in a 150°C/300°F/gas mark 2 oven for 3-4 hours.

# CHARLOTTE AUX FRUITS ROUGES DU SUNDGAU

### Red Fruit Mousse Moulded in Sponge Fingers

*This delicate and colourful dessert comes from Elizabeth Lacour, the talented British chef-pâtissière at the Restaurant La Couronne in Buschwiller. If you prefer, a crème anglaise (see right) can be made from the surplus egg yolks and served with the dessert in place of the raspberry coulis.*

**SERVES 6-8**
**24 sponge fingers (boudoir biscuits)**
**4tbsp caster sugar**
**1tbsp sweet liqueur such as *fraise*,**
***framboise* or Grand Marnier, optional**

**FOR THE COULIS**
**500g/18oz raspberries**
**150g/5oz sugar**

**FOR THE MOUSSE**
**6 sheets gelatine or 1tbsp powdered gelatine**
**400g/14oz raspberries or strawberries (or a mixture)**
**2tsp lemon juice**
**4 egg whites**
**50g/2oz caster sugar**
**250ml/8fl oz whipping cream**
**extra soft fruits and mint leaves, to garnish**

Halve enough sponge fingers to line the walls of a 24 or 29cm/9½or 10½in springform cake tin (6cm/2½in deep) and set them in the tin. Use the rest to line the bottom, cutting to fit. Dissolve the sugar in 4 tablespoons of water and add the liqueur, if using. Brush the sponge fingers with this syrup. To make the coulis, purée the raspberries with the sugar and push through a sieve to remove the pips. Spread about a quarter of the purée over the fingers in the bottom of the tin. Reserve the rest.

Soak the gelatine sheets in copious cold water until floppy. Squeeze them out and dissolve in 2 tablespoons of water over a gentle heat. If using powdered gelatine, sprinkle it onto 2-3 tablespoons of water in a small saucepan, leave until spongy, then dissolve thoroughly over a gentle heat. Purée the fruit for the mousse with the lemon juice in a liquidizer or food processor. Add the hot melted gelatine, then liquidize or process till smooth. Strain the purée.

Beat the egg whites into soft peaks, sprinkle on the sugar and continue beating to a stiff, meringue-like consistency. Whip the cream to soft peaks. Fold together the meringue, purée and cream using a large wire whisk. Pour into the prepared tin and smooth the top. Chill until firm.

Unmould the dessert, decorate with soft fruit and mint leaves. Serve the rest of the coulis or the *crème anglaise* separately.

# CREME ANGLAISE

### Real Custard or Vanilla Sauce

*Crème anglaise, a soothing, silky smooth sauce made with egg yolks, milk, sugar and vanilla, is not specifically alsacien (nor especially anglaise), but it is frequently served in Alsace as an accompaniment for desserts. It is important not to allow the sauce to boil, otherwise it will curdle. In place of the vanilla, orange or lemon zest, blackcurrant, lemon balm or mint leaves, elderflowers or cinnamon could be used to flavour the sauce.*

**MAKES ABOUT 500ML/16FL OZ SAUCE**
**500ml/16fl oz full cream milk**
**1 vanilla pod, split lengthwise or 2 pinches powdered vanilla or 1tsp vanilla extract**
**6 egg yolks**
**75-100g/3-3½oz caster sugar**

Heat the milk to boiling in a double saucepan with the vanilla pod, powder or extract. Beat the yolks and sugar together until light and fluffy. Add the boiling milk and beat well to mix. Return everything to the pan and stir over a gentle heat until wisps of steam appear. To test if the custard is ready, lift the spoon from the mixture and let it cool for a minute, then run your finger over the back of the spoon: a channel should be formed. Do not let it come near to boiling or you will scramble it. Strain the sauce into a bowl, cool, then chill.

# TARTE AU FROMAGE BLANC

## Alsatian Cheesecake

*Cheesecake in Alsace is light and delicate, made simply with* fromage blanc, *cream, eggs, sugar and a hint of lemon zest, and baked in a pastry shell. A deep red fruit coulis (see page 102) goes well with it. (Illustrated above)*

**SERVES 8**
**FOR THE PASTRY**
**200g/7oz plain flour**
**100g/3 ½oz unsalted butter**

**FOR THE FILLING**
**4 eggs, separated**
**100g/3 ½oz caster sugar**
**500g/18oz *fromage blanc* (40% fat content)**
**200ml/7fl oz whipping cream**
**2tbsp cornflour**
**pinch of salt**
**icing sugar, for dusting**

To make the pastry, sift the flour into a mixing bowl or the goblet of a food processor. Cut the butter into small pieces, add to the bowl and blend until the mixture resembles fine crumbs. Add 7 teaspoons of iced water and process to a dough. Wrap the pastry in film and refrigerate.

Preheat the oven to 180°C/350°F/gas mark 4. Roll out the pastry to fit a 30cm/12in loose-bottomed quiche tin.

In a large bowl or a food processor, mix together the egg yolks, half of the sugar, the *fromage blanc*, cream and cornflour. Beat the egg whites with the salt to soft peaks, sprinkle on the remaining sugar and continue beating until stiff. Fold them into the *fromage blanc* mixture. Turn into the pastry case and bake near the bottom of the oven for 35-40 minutes or until golden brown and a skewer inserted in the middle comes out clean.

Place a sheet of greaseproof paper on top of the cheesecake, invert it onto a rack then unmould it. Inverting stops any excess liquid in the fromage blanc from seeping into the pastry and making it soggy. When cool, set right side up on your best plate and sprinkle with icing sugar. Serve at room temperature with the coulis.

*FAR RIGHT Cow bells hang from the beams
of a ferme-auberge in the Vosges.
The smaller ones are worn by the cows when
they are taken up to the hill farm from
the valley in May, and again for the descent to
the village in September.
RIGHT A small restaurant with rooms in
Kaysersberg at the foot of the Vosges, owned
by a former champion cyclist.
BELOW A classic view of the Vosges.*

# THE VOSGES

Driving up into the Vosges from the plain of Alsace, it is difficult to believe that one is still in the same province, so dramatically different is the landscape. Quite abruptly the neatly contoured vineyards give way to wide sunlit valleys and tumbling streams, steeply banked forests of beech and pine and windswept upland meadows above the tree line. In place of tightly clustered, solidly built salmon- and ochre-washed houses come lone, long, low farm buildings, whitewashed with grey slate roofs. The roasting summer temperatures that ripen the grapes on the vineyard slopes drop rapidly as one climbs. An apparently mild spring day in the plain shows its true winter colours up on the Route des Crêtes.

The Alps, by their sheer size and scale, are awe-inspiring; the volcanic peaks of the Auvergne are stern and grey-faced; the Black Forest range (the mirror image of the Vosges and once part of the same *massif*) is clothed in dark pine woods. But the Vosges are manageable mountains, the highest scarcely reaching 1500 metres (around 5000 feet). The forests are mixed broadleaf and evergreen which gives them a light and lacy look in spring and makes for superb autumnal colours. The hillside pastures are lush and green in summer against a misty blue backdrop of endlessly unfolding peaks.

The climate is typical of all mountain regions: rough, ready and unpredictable. The Vosges act as a sort of wind- and rain-break, and the storm clouds looming in from the west dump their contents all along the mountain range, leaving the plain of Alsace warm, sheltered and relatively dry. Rainfall up on the Hohneck is four times that of Colmar, not forty kilometres (twenty-five miles) away. Essential prerequisites for sorties into the hills are good clothing and footwear, serious walking maps, well-warmed muscles – and a hearty appetite, for this is the land of the *ferme-auberge* (see page 107) and prime picnicking terrain.

The area has always been relatively poor. In the early days cattle grazing and cheese making, logging and charcoal burning were the principal activities. Later textile manufacture and mining provided valuable employment in the valleys. Nowadays the emphasis is all on *le tourisme vert* – active outdoor holidays with mild ecological overtones. Walkers are particularly well catered for: some 11,000 kilometres (nearly 7,000 miles) of walking paths, the whole length of Alsace from Wissembourg to Ferrette, have been mapped out and marked by the redoubtable Club Vosgien. Several *Grandes Randonnées* (long-distance hiking trails that criss-cross France) pass through the region. Cross-country skiing trails and a few lifts for (novice) downhill skiers come into their own when snow conditions permit.

Though poor from an economic point of view, the Vosges have immense wealth in the ecological sense. Highland pastures (*les hautes chaumes*), fields of wild gentians and pansies, ancient peat bogs disturbed only by the laughing chatter of little grebes, woodland banks of bilberries and mountain cranberries, solitary chamois, families of wild boar and the occasional roe deer, and distant views on clear autumn days into Germany, Switzerland and Lorraine: this is the rich heritage of the Vosges which is held dear by the *alsaciens*. For many of them the area is like a precious back yard which they wisely enjoy to the full – at weekends, on high days and holidays, on crisp snowy winter days when fresh air beckons and on stifling summer days when the heat in the plain becomes oppressive.

## THE BALLON D'ALSACE

When the Ballon d'Alsace, the southernmost peak in the Vosges, is visible from the Sundgau it is a sign to drop everything and hasten up into the hills. There are two reasons for this unseemly scramble: firstly, the views from the summit and of the whole Vosges chain to north and west across to the Black Forest – and, on exceptional days, of the Alps far to the south – must not be missed. Secondly, when the mountains are clear, it means that the wind is in the south-west and a change in the weather is imminent.

The Vallée de la Doller, which spreads itself out at the feet of the Ballon d'Alsace, is a friendly, wide-bottomed valley down which the eponymous river rattles busily, and upon whose banks a picnic rug can comfortably be spread. The products of Monsieur Bringel the butcher in Guewenheim would go a long way towards furnishing the picnic basket: *pâté en croûte*, *terrine maison*, a delicious lightly smoked beef sausage for eating raw, known as a *chasseur* (huntsman), and foie gras in various forms. Thanks to the Bringels' initiative in the mid-1980s, several families in the neighbourhood began to raise ducks and to fatten them for their livers, since when the area has obtained the label *Ballon d'Alsace – le Pays du Foie Gras*. (The name Ballon evokes the nicely rounded, ballooning shapes of the mountains.)

Sentheim is served in summer by a steam train which labours up and down from Cernay. The village baker makes a moist rye loaf with a chewy crust called a *Pavé de Sentheim*, proudly claimed by the baker's wife to be *'la monopole de la Vallée!'* The wine merchant Adam in Lauw, related to the famous wine-growing dynasty in Ammerschwihr, will provide a fresh and fruity Pinot Blanc from their amply furnished cellar. Picnic purchases can be completed in Masevaux, principal town of the Doller valley, famous for its Passion Play before Easter and its organ festival in August and September.

If the weather is unfriendly, lunch at the cunningly concealed Auberge du Schlumpf above the village of Dolleren may be indicated. It is one of the best kept secrets of the valley. The charming and solicitous *patronne*, Madame Behra, prefers discretion. On hearing the title of this book, she threw up her hands in horror. 'We don't really do "gastronomy" here,' she explained apologetically, 'just home cooking and local products – nothing fancy!' *Bouchée forestière* (a vol-au-vent packed with wild mushrooms), *pot-au-feu* and veal from the farm with home-made noodles are all candidates for the daily menu. Madame's *maman* prepares

*TOP A slice of* tourte *opens the classic* repas marcaire *(see page 107) at a* ferme-auberge *in the Vosges.*
*ABOVE Bringel the butcher and foie gras specialist in Guewenheim in the Vallée de la Doller.*
*OPPOSITE The Vosges near Lapoutroie.*

## FERMES-AUBERGES

*In the old days*, fermes-auberges, *many of them
accessible only on foot, offered simple
snacks to passing walkers.
Food was based on the farm's produce and
served on wooden trestle tables and
benches inside or outside the farmhouse.
Nowadays many are big enterprises with huge
car parks and fancy menus, though
a few have conserved their simple character.
Whatever the size or scale, in order to
qualify for the appellation today, a* ferme-
auberge *must be a working farm
and at least 70 per cent of the food must be
home grown. The typical meal, the* repas
marcaire *or 'dairyman's meal' consists of soup,
followed by a major portion of* tourte
*(a savoury pie of ground pork with pastry top
and bottom) served warm with salad.
Next comes sliced smoked pork shoulder
(*Schiffala*) with an irresistible - and
unpronounceable - confection known as*
Roïgabrageldi, *hash potatoes. Then comes
Munster or mountain cheese, often
home produced. The final nail in the coffin
is usually a fruit tart in season
served with lashings of whipped cream, or a*
méringue glacée *of heroic proportions.*

LEFT Monsieur Bruxer the butcher in
Kaysersberg brandishes a groaning board of his
own home-smoked and cured meats,
sausages, pâtés and terrines. A recent and
succulent creation of his is tenderloin of pork
cured in the smokery at the back of the shop.
RIGHT The river Doller tumbles down
the valley to the plain.
BELOW Walkers, cyclists and parapentists all
enjoy these sorts of views up on the Route
des Crêtes, the road along the top of the Vosges
that forms a kind of saddle and runs
between Cernay in the south and
the Col du Bonhomme.

# THE CHARCUTERIE OF
## ALSACE

Two things distinguish an Alsace butcher from
his confrères in the rest of France. First, in
Alsace the professions of boucher and charcutier
are combined, which means that he is a
specialist in both fresh and cured meats; the
other big difference lies in his magnificent range
of smoked meat products (les fumaisons)
which are the pride of any Alsace butcher
worthy of the name. Seemingly every part of the
pig is potential smokery material: loin (filet
or Kassler), shoulder (palette, Schiffala), neck
(collet), ham (jambon, Schunke), bacon
(lard, Speck) and many more. Of these pork
specialities, the ones to be eaten raw (e.g. jambon
cru, lard paysan) are dry-salted and cold-
smoked; pieces to be cooked (Kassler, Schiffala,
collet) are brined and then smoked using pine
sawdust and sometimes a few green pine
branches from the Vosges for extra flavour.
Then there are the sausages, made variously
from pork, beef, veal or a mixture. Some are
raw, others are cooked for eating cold in salads
or reheating to serve with potatoes. They may be
smoked or nature.

all food in or on the wood-fired stove that backs onto the dining room and sends out wonderful warm waves on a winter's day. From the windows there are views of the valley and of the many walking tracks which radiate out from the Auberge.

The road winds its way up towards the Ballon d'Alsace: views back down the valley are strictly for passengers, car drivers should concentrate their attention on the vagaries of the road, or pull off in order to enjoy them to the full. Even those cyclists not in training for the Tour de France will experience a sense of real achievement and power at reaching the top. Down the other side, the See d'Urbés outside St Maurice-sur-Moselle, one of Alsace's few remaining peat bogs, is a place of desolate beauty. Now a nature reserve, it is intersected by a network of paths equipped with explanation boards identifying the precious flora and fauna that flourish here. Little grebes, mallards, herons, water hens and teal skitter about among the stumps that stick out of the peaty water.

Close by, in Storkensohn, a group of villagers recently resurrected the old oil mill to which families would bring their shelled walnuts for grinding. The rustic mill holds demonstrations during the summer, and by special request for groups. Further down the valley is the town of St Amarin, scene of a spectacular midsummer bonfire (Les Feux de la Saint Jean). The town gives its name to the Val St Amarin, the north–south valley that links it with Wildenstein, and an important southern focus of Munster cheese production. The Route Joffre is a picturesque road built in the First World War to link the Doller and Thur valleys.

# THE GRAND BALLON

Further north is the Grand Ballon, the highest peak in the Vosges at 1424 metres (4672 feet), reached via the Route des Crêtes which starts close to Cernay, at Uffholtz. There are not many reasons for visiting Cernay but a pit stop at the Boucherie-Charcuterie chez Alain for picnic provisions for a hike or a day's cross-country skiing is certainly one of them. '*Gourmet, averti, exigeant: tel est le client que nous aimons!*' ('Discerning, well informed and demanding – that's how we like our customers!') is the house maxim.

From Uffholtz the road zigzags alarmingly up the Route des Crêtes through a series of *cols* or passes to the foot of the Grand Ballon. At the Col du Silberloch one of Alsace's many sobering memorial graveyards looks towards the hill of Hartmanswillerkopf, in the battles for which some 30,000 French and German soldiers lost their lives in the First World War. (The name was clearly too much of a mouthful for the French 'squaddies', who nicknamed it Le Vieil-Armand.) The walking possibilities around here are inexhaustible, and the views of peak after peak succeeding one another into the distance are breathtaking.

At the Ferme-Auberge Molkenrain the Deybach family holds an annual *fête de la transhumance*, when the cows are taken up to their summer quarters. At around lunch time on the appointed day in May the herd is assembled down in the village of Wattwiller to embark on their three-hour climb, accompanied by a happy throng of hangers-on of all ages. Once up at the farm the cows career around the fields like children let out of school, and the walkers pile inside to enjoy their evening meal.

*TOP Mushrooming in the Vosges is a favourite pastime during the summer and autumn months. Here the basket contains mainly field mushrooms, but chanterelles, cepes and horns of plenty are also to be found. ABOVE Walkers stride out on a sunny day. Paths in the Vosges are clearly signposted with a series of colour-coded symbols, with helpful indications of distance to the next landmark, village or ferme-auberge.*

LEFT *This wrought-iron sign shows two local specialities: the* bretzel *and the* Kougelhopf.
BELOW LEFT *The main street of Niedermorschwihr, home of Christine Ferber (top far left), is particularly well endowed with colourful half-timbered houses. Shades of brown, ochre and salmon are commonplace, and blue (traditionally the colour of the Virgin, and therefore typical of Catholic villages) is also found.*
BELOW *Cowbells at the Ferme-Auberge Buchwald. Monsieur Wehrey and his family still take the cows up on foot from the valley to the farm and back down again in the autumn.*

## LES CONFITURES DE CHRISTINE FERBER

*A jam session at Christine Ferber's is an unforgettable experience. Row upon row of bonneted and beribboned jam pots line the shelves in her shop on the main street of Niedermorschwihr in the foothills of the Vosges. Though the production – and above all the range – of her jams is nowadays considerable, Madame Ferber is determined to preserve the artisanal nature of the business. All jams are prepared from mostly local fruits in the same copper pans that her mother once used; only the recipes have been modified to reduce the traditional one-to-one ratio of sugar to fruit to between 650 and 800 grammes of sugar per kilo of fruit, depending on the type and its degree of ripeness. To the range of jams and jellies (rhubarb, sour cherry with mint, raspberry with lemon balm, bilberry, mountain cranberry, quetsch plums, mirabelle, blackberry, crab apple, rosehip, quince...) have now been added a selection of sweet-sour preserves and confits. These include apricots or mirabelles in Gewurztraminer, tomatoes with herbs and pêches des vignes poached in Pinot Noir.*

At Le Markstein (scene of many a novice skier's first laborious snow-plough turns) the road turns into the Florival or valley of flowers. To one side of it is the tiny village of Murbach with its Romanesque abbey, whose now truncated remains (only the chancel stands) give little clue to its once vast scope and influence. Founded in the eighth century by St Pirmin, the abbey became a famous Benedictine centre of learning, enjoyed the personal protection of Charlemagne and dominated the valley of Guebwiller for close to ten centuries.

Among its extensive possessions were some of the prime vineyards of Alsace, including those which rise above Guebwiller. After the Revolution the abbey was sacked, its land and belongings scattered. At the beginning of this century the famous wine-growing family Schlumberger patiently began to buy up all the steeply terraced vineyards formerly owned by the abbey and to replant them with 'noble' varieties. Today the Domaines Schlumberger pay homage to the abbots with their superb Riesling and Gewurztraminer des Princes-Abbés.

Guebwiller, a solidly built, pink sandstone town with some fine churches, sits at the foot of the Florival. Saint-Léger is one of the Romanesque treasures of Alsace, completed in about 1235 by masons whose meagre diet was chronicled to have been unlimited garlic and bread. Only on Sundays were they allowed to break their fast and treat themselves to a little meat. Lunch in the next-door Taverne du Vigneron or tea at the renowned café and pastry shop Christmann will provide sustenance of a more self-indulgent sort.

The smiling valley of Rimbach is reached via Soultz, whose wonderful main square (scene of a good Wednesday market) is surrounded by fine old houses with some good oriel windows. On the rue Maréchal de Lattre the redoubtable Monsieur Schluraff, known far and wide for his impressive girth, holds sway in his S'Metzgerstuwa. A restaurant and butcher's shop, it is something of a pilgrimage site for serious carnivores (a species which is still fairly common in Alsace). Organic meat and *charcuterie* are the specialities of the Boucherie Schellenberger on the same street.

A couple of peaceful hotels (in Michelin's red rocking chair category) at Thierenbach cater for the needs of pilgrims and other passers-by, while another road leads up to Rimbach at the foot of the Grand Ballon. At the head of the valley is the Ferme-Auberge Glashütte, where the first to ring and book earns the right to choose the menu. Madame Christmann's *Bouchées à la Reine* (impressive vol-au-vents of chicken and mushrooms in a creamy sauce, see recipe page 99) is frequently top of the request list, as is her *tourte*, a deep and satisfying plate pie which is a meal in itself.

# THE MUNSTER VALLEY

In the heart of the Hautes Vosges is the Munster valley, epicentre of *ferme-auberge* country and spiritual home of the remarkable cheese whose name it shares. Between Turckheim and Gunsbach (where Albert Schweitzer lived for many years and his father was pastor), the vines which line the north side of the road give way to walnut trees and fruit orchards. To the south of the valley the hills are thickly wooded and rise up towards the Petit Ballon, the last of the three Ballons.

## JEAN-PAUL GILG, MAITRE PATISSIER-CHOCOLATIER-GLACIER

*The Gilg pastry shop, founded in 1938 by grandfather Gilg, is a legend throughout Alsace. Countless apprentice pastry chefs and chocolatiers have been formed here, and the years have seen an endless succession of elegantly wrapped and boxed breads, cakes, chocolates and desserts emerging through its doors. The shop's beautiful façade is embellished with a marvellous sculpted pâtissier diving out of an upstairs window in pursuit of a disappearing Kougelhopf. Besides a classic selection of pralines, fruit tarts, sweet and savoury Kougelhopfs and chocolate cakes to die for, there are house creations such as Le Délice du Marcaire, a walnut and almond tart with pastry top and bottom, and Le Petit Munster, a round box of the dimensions of a Munster cheese containing dark chocolates with an almond and Marc de Gewurztraminer filling. There is a café adjacent to the shop and, in summer, tables spill joyfully out onto the pavement.*

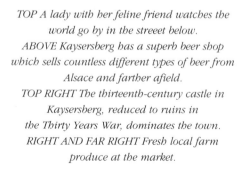

TOP A lady with her feline friend watches the
world go by in the streeet below.
ABOVE Kaysersberg has a superb beer shop
which sells countless different types of beer from
Alsace and farther afield.
TOP RIGHT The thirteenth-century castle in
Kaysersberg, reduced to ruins in
the Thirty Years War, dominates the town.
RIGHT AND FAR RIGHT Fresh local farm
produce at the market.

*BOTTOM Kaysersberg marks the transition from Vosges to vineyards. Here the river Weiss rattles down through the town.*
*BELOW A picture of the Virgin is captured in the angle between two houses in Kaysersberg.*

The Ferme-Auberge Buchwald is a huge and friendly place with outstanding views from the perennially packed dining room. From the beams on the ceiling hang great burnished bells worn by the cows when they come up to their summer pastures around the feast of St Urbain (25 May), and for their descent to the village again at Michaelmas (25 September). The welcome from the Kempf family at the bottom of the extremely bumpy forest track which leads to the cosy little Ferme-Auberge Lameysberg is equally friendly, the *repas marcaire* (see page 107) one of the best available, and Monsieur Kempf's Munster (which you can watch him making) well made and properly aged.

The town of Munster, founded by Irish monks in the seventh century, was once a prosperous textile centre and nowadays thrives on tourism. The Grand'rue is lined with shops selling walking sticks and maps, guide books to the best *fermes-auberges*, freshly roasted coffee, picnic provisions, backpacks and bilberry tarts. The Dischinger family shop sells cheese from the Ferme-Auberge Christlesgut (see below), wines, *eaux-de-vie*, hams and sausages, any of which can be vacuum-packed for transportation. Among the specialities of the Boucherie-Charcuterie Jacquat is La Canne du Marcaire. Shaped like a little walking stick, it is a smoked sausage that can be nibbled to stave off the hunger pangs if those last thirty minutes to the next *ferme-auberge* should seem endless.

Also on the main street is Monsieur Wendling the game specialist. In Alsace the season opens in April for wild boar and in May for roe deer, but his busiest period (for both direct sales and mail order) is between September and January. Controls are getting tighter all the time: game may no longer be sold still clothed in its fur or feathers; the days of magnificent shop window displays of wild boar with wiry coat, snout, tail and trotters intact, or pheasants complete with their beautiful plumage, are undoubtedly numbered.

The Ferme-Auberge Christlesgut above Breitenbach is reached by an increasingly rocky road. The Dischinger family's excellent farmhouse Munsters (*Munster fermier*) and mountain cheese (*Barikas*) are to be found in markets from Sélestat to Mulhouse as well as in Monsieur Dischinger *frère's* shop in Munster. Some of the farm's herby mountain cheese goes into one of the Auberge's house specialities: *Steakäs* or *beignets de fromage*, consisting of thick slices of mountain cheese dipped in a light crêpe batter and pan-fried. Served with salad they make a wonderful walker's lunch.

Mulhbach's Musée de la Schlitte is superbly conceived and maintained and its contents are beautifully presented. Members of the founding association take turns to guide visitors around the display of artefacts and photographs depicting the life of local woodcutters in the (not so distant) days when firewood was brought down from the steep forests by sledge (*Schlitte*) on specially constructed wooden sled runs.

From here onwards up the Munster valley *fermes-auberges* start to succeed one another thick and fast: Braunkopf, Hinterberg, Schiessroth and Gaschney. For those more inclined towards *les provisions tirées du sac* (provisions from the backpack), the banks of the infant river Fecht in the Sondernach valley are tailor-made for picnicking.

Up on the Route des Crêtes the parapentists wheel and circle like great exotic birds of prey; mountain bikers pound relentlessly onwards and upwards; walkers amble amiably along endless paths and tracks. The Kastelberg farm has some of the best views and – some

*TOP RIGHT Fruit tarts of all sorts are a favourite dessert or tea-time treat in Alsace.*
*This one, a tarte aux quetsches (plum tart), is made in the autumn with the blue-black plums that are typical of the region, bound together with a creamy custard.*
*The ornately decorated wine cooler doubles up beautifully as a vase.*
*ABOVE RIGHT Illuminated booths create a wonderful atmosphere at the picturesque Kaysersberg Christmas market.*
*ABOVE Kaysersberg is almost more magical by night than by day, particularly when decorated for Christmas.*

claim – the finest *Roïgabrageldi* (hash potatoes) in the Munster valley. The Jardin d'Altitude du Haut Chitelet on the crest, owned by the botanic gardens of Nancy, is an oasis of calm where alpine plants (both local and otherwise) are set in their natural habitat. The road down the Col de la Schlucht, built in 1860 by the Hartmann family from Munster, leads back to the town again.

## LES TROIS VALLEES

Continuing our journey northwards through the Vosges, we come upon the three valleys that combine to market their undoubted appeal under the label of Les Trois Vallées: Lapoutroie, Ste Marie-aux-Mines (alias the Val d'Argent) and Orbey. The remarkable old town of Kaysersberg makes the bridge between vineyards and Vosges and provides the opening to this lovely area. Birthplace of Albert Schweitzer and the scene in December of a magical

Christmas market, the town has attracted a number of craftspeople making high quality goods such as pottery (similar to that of Soufflenheim, see page 21, with softer colours and more appealing designs) and wooden toys.

On the outskirts is the Clos des Capucins, the beautiful property of Madame Faller and her daughters whose voluptuous wines are world famous. On the picturesque main street the Pâtisserie Loecken makes the best *Kougelhopf* in Alsace (both sweet and savoury varieties), while the genial Monsieur Bruxer – Madame Faller's favourite butcher – makes a number of smoked specialities, notably a succulent *filet mignon de porc fumé* (smoked tenderloin of pork) and some tasty little bundles of smoked beef sausages called *fagots du vigneron*.

Up the valley at Hachimette (just past the revamped railway carriage, festooned with geraniums, which houses the Tourist Bureau) is an excellent shop called Le Cellier des Montagnes. Run by the Coopérative Agricole du Canton Vert – an apt name for this verdant valley – it sells Munster, goats' and mountain cheese, butter and other dairy products, poultry and free range eggs, honey, jam and a superb selection of fresh and smoked meats and smoked trout. A vacuum-packing service is provided at the shop for easy transportation of purchased goodies.

Lapoutroie has a number of decent hotels, a great *affineur* of Munster cheeses, Jacques Haxaire, and two distillers, Miclo and de Miscault, the latter responsible for the instructive Musée des Eaux-de-vie. The Ferme-Auberge Kébespré, high above the town, is a perfect choice for Sunday lunch on Mother's Day. The tables have special posies for *maman*, the deliciously kitsch and cosy wood-panelled dining room reverberates with the sound of happy families indulging in Madame Verchère's legendary food: the classic *repas marcaire* (see page 107) or a dish of slowly braised, milk-fed veal from the farm.

From Le Bonhomme another dramatic road snakes its way up to the Col des Bagenelles. A panorama of the Val d'Argent opens up on all sides: to north, south, east and west is a vista of unfolding hills and green valleys. The Ferme-Auberge le Haycot offers a good lunch and maps with suggestions for wonderful walks all around the area of Le Brézouard. From the Col des Bagenelles a delightful road leads down the valley alongside the dancing river Liépvrette to Ste Marie-aux-Mines, formerly a silver-mining town and textile centre.

As the road climbs out of the valley again there is a sign to Ribeauvillé. The Ferme-Auberge du Petit-Haut, run by the young Mathieu family, is another establishment with superb views, good food and a few simple rooms. A right turn just after the farm leads down a spectacular road to Aubure and Fréland, where the Maison du Pays Welche can be found. The etymology of '*welche*' combines the concepts both of 'foreign' and 'French-speaking', and the museum is dedicated to the traditions (linguistic and other) of this little French-speaking enclave surrounded on all sides by dialect speakers.

The modest little town of Orbey leads to the third of the valleys, the Val d'Orbey. The specialist dairyman and cheese maker Patrick Chaize, purveyor of Munster and other cheeses to Jacky Quesnot in Colmar, is found on the way up to Basses Huttes, while further on is the Ferme du Pré du Bois (see page 117). The worthwhile museum and the battlefield of the Linge, a sobering memorial of the First World War, should not be missed, after which lunch at the Ferme-Auberge Glasborn-Linge nearby provides a welcome change of mood.

*TOP A bird's eye view of the little village of Hohrod, above the town of Munster – note the distant snow-capped peaks in the background. Parts of the Route des Crêtes in the high Vosges are closed from around November till April or May depending on snow conditions.*
*ABOVE Fruit picking in the Vosges. Some of the fruit is used for cooking or for preserves, but the lion's share goes into the still to make the pungent clear white spirits for which Alsace is famous. As the right to distil dies out, so also the trees fall sadly into disrepair, left untended and unpruned.*

## EAUX-DE-VIE

*The powerful, intensely aromatic fruit spirits of Alsace in their slim, elegant bottles must count among the region's greatest specialities. Many locally grown fruits, notably cherries, raspberries, quetsch plums and mirabelles, are distilled here. Marc, the residue left after grape pressing and furnished by the nearby vineyards, is also distilled to give a spirit of the same name.*
*Eau-de-vie de Poire Williams has been perfected by Alsace distillers, though the pears come generally from the Rhône valley. There is also a strictly local range of indigenous wild flowers and berries, including woodruff, wild service berry, hollyberry, sloe, elderflower and bilberry, which are used to make all manner of weird and wonderful* eau-de-vie. *Curiouser and curiouser are the spirits distilled from asparagus, beer,* choucroute *or cumin.*
*Sugar-rich stone fruits (*les fruits à noyau*) are first fermented, then distilled. Berries and plants that do not contain enough sugar to ferment spontaneously are macerated in grape brandy before distilling. All Alsace fruit spirits are clear, dry, aromatic and powerful (the optimum alcohol content is considered to be 45 per cent), whilst fruit liqueurs, intensely sweet and coloured with the juice of the fruit from which they are made, are somewhat lower in alcohol.*
*In the past the right to distil a limited amount of spirits privately for home consumption without paying tax was passed down from generation to generation. This right will die out with today's Alsatian grandparents, and the days of the* bouilleur de cru *or home distiller are numbered. In the Val de Villé professional distillers are still fairly numerous: some, like the Meyer family in Hohwarth, are equipped with the very latest technology Some of their stunning* eaux-de-vie *are presented in eminently collectable, hand-blown glass bottles (like those pictured left) which are on sale in the elegantly panelled shop and tasting room on the main street of the village.*

# THE VAL DE VILLE

Finally comes the Val de Villé, one of the loveliest and least visited parts of the Vosges foothills. Here in the north the peaks are softer, the outlines more rounded, the passes lower. The whole area is a glorious sight in springtime, ablaze with cherry, plum, mirabelle and apple blossom, and also in the autumn when the fruits hang heavy on the branches.

The little town of Villé is the focal point for the area: all roads seem to lead here. The Wednesday morning market brings in farmers' wives from a number of surrounding villages with their hand-patted butter, *fromage blanc*, crème fraîche, yogurts, flans and free-range eggs. The area is full of cottages and rooms to let, bed-and-breakfasts, farms offering riding holidays and home-grown *produits du terroir*. In the lovely village of Albé, once a major wine-growing commune, the Maison du Val de Villé retraces the rich heritage of this once prosperous valley with its history of mining and textiles.

The drive up to the Col du Kreuzweg affords wonderful views to every side: closely mown hillsides dotted with wild cherries alternate with dense and stately pine forests. The once-fashionable resort of Le Hohwald is now a tranquil backwater, a favourite walking and bilberry-picking spot for weekending *Strasbourgeois* who settle down on the terrace of La Petite Auberge to catch their breath, quench their thirst and tuck into a *mousse de truite fumée*, a dish of game or a *tarte aux myrtilles*. On the edge of the village at the rustic and delightful Ferme-Auberge du Wittertalhof Madame Hazemann and her daughter serve *plats du jour* made from their own farm produce.

Down a bumpy track off the road between the Col de la Charbonnière and the Col de Steige is to be found some of the finest food in the Vosges: at the Ferme Promont Madame Schynoll's cooking, based on home-raised meat (lamb, veal, rabbit, pork) and other products from the farm, is a superb example of what can be done with first-class, fresh ingredients, considerable culinary skill and the great gift of simplicity. In the autumn people beat a path to her door for the famous *repas cochonailles* (a meal which revolves entirely around the products of the autumnal slaughtering). Bookings – in any case essential – are made months ahead for the traditional menu of soup, *boudin* (black pudding), pig's feet and other delights, served up with lashings of salad and *choucroute*, and accompanied by an orchestra to ensure the right ambiance.

At La Salcée (so named because of its position in ancient times on the *route du sel* that linked the salt mines of Lorraine with Alsace) is the wonderful family business Les Confitures du Climont. Owned and run by the Krencker family, one of the brothers gave up a career as a primary schoolteacher to concentrate on making jams and preserves. The didactic spirit lives on, and he gives spirited and humorous demonstrations of the preserving process, spiked with interesting titbits of information and questions to 'students'. Some of the jams are made from locally grown fruits, others grow wild in the forests and fields; all can be tasted in the parlour. To the north the Vallée de la Bruche, which links Molsheim with Saales, is the last major valley intersecting the Vosges until the Col de Saverne cuts through it further north. Gradually the typical landscape of the *Vosges alsaciens* begins to cede and the influence of neighbouring Lorraine becomes increasingly evident.

*The Maire family make magnificent Munsters at the Ferme du Pré du Bois near Orbey. The herd is milked early in the morning and at 10.30 a.m. Madame Maire makes a start on the cheese. Rennet is added to the warm milk, the curds form and are scooped into moulds. Once set, the cheeses are turned, sprinkled with coarse salt on both sides, washed and dried. They then descend to the dairy to ripen for at least three weeks —though three to four are best, considers Madame Maire.*

# FERME-AUBERGE IRRKRUT

**COL DE FOUCHY, 67220 VILLE, TEL 88 57 09 29**

*Noëlle and Michel Nell at the Ferme-Auberge Irrkrüt are no ordinary* Baribüre *(hill farmers).
Michel was born in Alsace and studied at the agricultural college in Obernai. Noëlle, of both
Norman and Périgord stock, is an accomplished artist, a skilled horsewoman – and a
terrific cook. Together they bought the farm in 1988 (the name, roughly translated, refers to
the 'crazy herbs' which were supposed to grow nearby) and stocked it with sheep, some cows,
ducks, chickens and a fiercely French* cochon gaulois *called Vercingetorix. Rabbits and
guinea fowl dip in and out of the menagerie at different moments. The atmosphere at Irrkrüt
is relaxed and joyous, people seem to turn up at all times of the day and the welcome is always
warm whatever the hour. The food is fun and different – a far cry from the usual*
ferme-auberge *fare. The couple recently won a national award for their* produits alimentaires
de montagne – *smoked leg of lamb, mountain ham, wild boar ham, smoked duck breast, foie
gras, bacon and various terrines, many of which can be purchased to take away.*

## TOURTE IRRKRUT AU MUNSTER

### *Irrkrüt's Munster Cheese Pie with Bacon and Potatoes*

*This delicious dish typifies Noëlle Nell's cuisine, which has been described as 'inventive cooking based on local specialities'. Her* tourte *contains Munster cheese, potatoes and bacon instead of the traditional pork filling (see page 124). It makes a wonderful, robust lunch or supper dish with salad. (Illustrated opposite)*

**SERVES 8**
**FOR THE PASTRY**
**250g/9oz plain flour**
**75g/3oz salted butter**
**50g/2oz margarine**
**pinch of salt**

**FOR THE FILLING**
**4 large waxy potatoes, peeled and sliced**
**(about 1kg/2 ¼ lb)**
**milk, to cover potatoes**
**2 onions, finely sliced**
**2 tbsp goose or duck fat (or oil)**
**2 well-ripened Munster cheeses, sliced**
**100g/3 ½ oz lardons**
**lots of parsley**
**300g/10oz bought puff pastry**
**1 egg yolk, diluted with a little water**
**sesame seeds, optional**
**salt and freshly ground black pepper**

Make up the pastry with the flour, salt, butter, margarine and cold water according to your own preferred pastry method or as instructed on page 124. Wrap it in cling film or foil and refrigerate while you cook the potatoes.

Place the sliced potatoes in a non-stick saucepan, cover with milk and simmer for 10-15 minutes or until just tender. Preheat the oven to 220°F/425°F/gas mark 7. Butter a 30cm/12in loose-bottomed quiche tin. Roll out the shortcrust pastry to a circle large enough to line the tin and give a 2cm/¾in border. Arrange the pastry in the tin and trim with scissors to leave a 2cm/¾in border. Heat the fat or oil and fry the onions until lightly golden, then spread them over the pastry. Arrange slices of Munster all over and sprinkle the lardons on top. Cover with the potatoes, salt and pepper to taste and chopped parsley.

Roll out the puff pastry to a circle the same size as before. Brush the shortcrust border with water, lay the puff pastry on top and trim to the same size as the shortcrust. Press the edges together to seal. Turn the border in on top of the pie to form a rolled edge. Make cross-hatchings in the pie top with the point of a sharp knife, paint with the diluted egg yolk and sprinkle with sesame seeds, if using.

Bake the *tourte* in the lower part of the oven for 45 minutes or until golden brown and hot through. If the top pastry is getting too brown, cover with foil.

## CLAFOUTIS AUX POIRES ET AU GINGEMBRE

### *Pear and ginger batter pudding*

*A simple and delicious late summer pudding in which the pears are subtly flavoured with ginger. Vanilla ice cream served with this pudding makes a nice cool contrast.*

**SERVES 6**
**4 well-flavoured dessert pears, peeled, quartered and cored**

**200g/7oz sugar**
**2 fingernail-sized pieces of zest and the juice of 1 lemon**
**6 eggs**
**100g/3 ½oz flour**
**250ml/8fl oz milk**
**1 tbsp *eau-de-vie* (preferably pear), optional**
**1 tsp ground ginger**
**or a walnut-sized piece fresh ginger, peeled and grated**
**4-5 tbsp ground hazelnuts or almonds**

Make a syrup by dissolving half the sugar in 500ml/16fl oz water with the lemon juice and zest and simmering for 5 minutes. Poach the pears in it for about 10 minutes or until just tender when pierced with a knife. Lift them out and cut into cubes. Discard the syrup.

In a food processor, blender or mixing bowl, mix together to a smooth batter the eggs, the remaining sugar, flour, milk, *eau-de-vie* (if used) and ginger. Let the batter rest for about an hour. Stir in the pear cubes.

Heat the oven to 200°C/400°F/gas mark 6. Butter an oval ovenproof dish approximately 35 x 20cm/14 x 8in and at least 5cm/2in deep. Sprinkle the ground hazelnuts or almonds all over the base and sides of the dish. Pour in the batter and bake the pudding for 35–40 minutes or until golden brown and well risen.

## MOUSSELINE DE POISSONS FUMES

### Mousseline of Smoked Salmon and Trout

*Throughout the Vosges there are pisciculteurs some of whom smoke their own fish. This rich and delicious layered terrine of smoked salmon and trout, which is best made the night before, is ideal for a first course or as part of a cold buffet. Serve with a light, lemony herb sauce cupped in a lettuce leaf. An alternative sauce would be a little horseradish cream mixed with lemon juice and whipped cream or Greek yogurt. (Illustrated above)*

**MAKES 14-16 SLICES**
**1 pkt (15g/ ½ oz) gelatine or aspic jelly**
**powder or 6 sheets of gelatine**
**250g/9oz smoked salmon**
**300g/10oz smoked trout**

**250ml/8fl oz whipping cream**
**salt and freshly ground black pepper**
**2tbsp mixed chopped chervil, parsley,**
**chives and tarragon**

**FOR THE SAUCE**
**zest of ½ lemon, cut into very thin strips**
**200ml/7fl oz whipping cream**
**2 tomatoes, peeled, seeded and diced**
**cayenne pepper**
**2tbsp chopped herbs as above**

**lettuce leaves, to garnish**
**sprigs of dill, to garnish**

Put 200ml/7fl oz of water in a saucepan, sprinkle over the gelatine or aspic powder and leave until spongy. If using gelatine sheets, soak them in copious cold water, squeeze out and add to the measured water. Heat gently to dissolve, stirring occasionally until clear.

Reserve 2-3 slices of each type of smoked fish. Roughly chop the remaining smoked salmon and put it in the food processor with 2 tablespoons of cream and half the dissolved gelatine/aspic. Process until quite smooth. Stir in half of the chopped herbs and transfer the mixture into a bowl. Repeat with the remaining smoked trout, 2 more tablespoons of cream and the rest of the gelatine/aspic and herbs. Whip the remaining cream until fairly stiff and divide it between the two fish preparations, folding it in carefully with a metal spoon. Season with pepper, taste and add salt if necessary.

Lightly oil an 8cm/3in deep, 26 x 10cm/10 x 4in terrine or loaf tin. Put in half the smoked trout mousse and smooth with a spatula. Lay the reserved slices of smoked salmon on top. Cover with all of the smoked salmon mousse, then the reserved slices of smoked trout. Finish with the rest of the smoked trout mousse. Chill for several hours or overnight.

To make the sauce, blanch the lemon zest strips in boiling water for 5 minutes. Drain and refresh. Whip the cream until stiff and fold in the tomato flesh, cayenne pepper to taste and the chopped herbs. To serve, unmould the terrine by dipping the tin in warm water for a few seconds. Then turn out onto a flat plate and slice. Put the slices on individual plates and garnish with dill sprigs. Arrange a nicely cupped lettuce leaf on each plate and spoon in some sauce.

# OMELETTE AU LARD OU AU JAMBON

## *Bacon or Ham Omelette*

*This* ferme-auberge *staple is simple and good, especially if your bacon or ham is nice and smoky. You can also add leftover* choucroute *to the omelette. To make an* omelette paysanne, *serve with cubes of potato fried up with chopped onion. Accompany with seasonal mixed salad leaves such as curly endive, lamb's lettuce and dandelion.*

**SERVES 2**
**100g/3 ½ oz lardons or thickly sliced ham cut in cubes**
**25g/1oz unsalted butter**
**5-6 eggs**
**2tbsp milk, water or beer**
**salt and freshly ground black pepper**
**seasonal salad leaves, to serve**

Put the lardons in a heavy omelette pan and cook them gently till the fat runs and they are lightly golden. Remove them with a slotted spoon and discard the excess fat from the pan. Return the pan to the heat, put in the butter and heat until foaming.

Meanwhile beat the eggs vigorously with the milk, water or beer (for lightness). Season carefully, having regard to the saltiness of the bacon, and pour the eggs into the omelette pan. When the bottom has set a little, put the lardons or ham cubes in a line down the middle. Cook for a further minute, or until the omelette is just set.

Fold a third of the omelette into the centre, then fold the other side over the top, to form a classic omelette shape. Alternatively, roll up your omelette from one side of the pan. Serve at once on heated plates.

# SALADE DE POMMES DE TERRE AUX LARDONS

## *Potato Salad with Lardons and Mustard Dressing*

*A well-made potato salad is irresistible at the best of times, but this version is particularly good. The lardons make a crusty contrast to the waxy potatoes in their sharp mustard dressing. In Alsace this salad is traditionally served with* charcuterie; *it is also excellent with barbecued meats.*

**SERVES 6**
**1kg/2 ¼ lb firm, waxy potatoes**
**125ml/4fl oz beef or chicken stock, hot**
**1 onion, finely chopped**
**lots of parsley, finely chopped**
**lots of chives, finely chopped**
**100g/3 ½ oz lardons**
**salt and freshly ground black pepper**

**FOR THE VINAIGRETTE**
**2tbsp French mustard**
**6tbsp olive oil**
**3tbsp dry white wine**
**3tbsp white wine vinegar**

Cook the potatoes in their skins in boiling salted water until just tender – about 20 minutes depending on their size. Peel while still warm (wear rubber gloves) and slice thickly. Put the slices of potato in a dish, pour on the hot stock and mix in the onion and herbs. Season to taste.

Fry the lardons gently till the fat runs and they are lightly golden. Mix together the vinaigrette ingredients and fold the lardons and vinaigrette into the potatoes. Serve the salad at room temperature.

## CHOU ROUGE A L'ALSACIENNE

### Red Cabbage with Apples and Red Wine

*An excellent dish, which should be prepared well in advance, to accompany game. Any leftovers improve on reheating. (Illustrated opposite, rear)*

SERVES 8

1 large red cabbage (about 1.5kg/3 ½ lb)
2tbsp caster sugar
200ml/7fl oz white wine vinegar
100g/3½ oz goose or duck fat or 5tbsp oil
1 onion, finely chopped
250ml/8fl oz red wine
250ml/8fl oz water or stock
1 bay leaf
2 cloves
2 tart apples such as Reinette,
Boskop or Bramley
salt and freshly ground black pepper

Cut the cabbage in half and remove the core. Slice the leaves thinly and wash in a colander. Shake dry. In a bowl, layer the sliced cabbage with the sugar, vinegar, salt and pepper. Leave for at least 1 hour and preferably overnight.

Heat the fat or oil in a large flameproof casserole and fry the onion gently until golden. Add the cabbage and its liquid, the red wine and water or stock. Tuck the bay leaf and cloves well down inside the casserole, cover and bring to the boil. Simmer very gently (or bake in the oven at 180°C/350°F/gas mark 4) for 1 ½ hours. Peel, core and chop the apples and add them to the casserole. Cook for a further 30 minutes. There should be hardly any liquid left at the end of the cooking time – if there is, boil it down hard to reduce.

## PETITS CHOUX FARCIS AUX OIGNONS ET AUX MARRONS

### Cabbage Parcels with Onions and Chestnuts

*This is another excellent dish to serve with game, and one that can be prepared in advance. (Illustrated opposite, centre)*

SERVES 10

10 large Savoy cabbage leaves
300g/10oz onions, finely chopped
50g/2oz butter
200g/7oz peeled chestnuts
200ml/7fl oz stock
2 egg yolks, lightly beaten
3tbsp whipping cream
wine glass of dry white wine
salt and freshly ground black pepper

Bring a large saucepan of salted water to the boil. Blanch the cabbage leaves for 5 minutes. Drain, refresh them in cold water, and dry them on a teatowel.

Heat the butter and soften the onions very gently until golden and fragrant. Stir in the chestnuts, add the stock, cover and cook gently for 20-25 minutes or until the chestnuts are just tender and the stock has evaporated. Do not overcook or they will disintegrate. Put the egg yolks and cream in a bowl and add the chestnuts. Mix to bind and season to taste.

Preheat the oven to 180°C/350°F/gas mark 4. Cut the hard central rib away from the cabbage leaves and put a tablespoon of filling on each leaf. Fold into parcels and place seam-side down, in a buttered ovenproof dish just big enough to take them in one layer. Pour over the wine, cover and bake for 30 minutes or until hot through.

## FLANS DE POTIRON

### Pumpkin Custards

*Ideal to serve as an accompaniment to duck, game or roast meat, this pumpkin custard can be baked in either a single soufflé dish or 6–8 individual ramekins. If you use the latter, you will need to turn them out on to plates to serve. (Illustrated opposite, left and right)*

SERVES 6-8

800g/1 ¾ lb slice of pumpkin
25g/1oz unsalted butter
3 eggs, beaten
200ml/7fl oz whipping cream
some grated nutmeg
finely grated zest of 1 orange
salt and freshly ground black pepper

Remove the skin and seeds from the pumpkin and chop the flesh roughly. Melt the butter in a saucepan, add the pumpkin and stew it for 20 minutes. Raise the heat and cook briskly, then remove the pan from the heat and mash the stewed pumpkin with a potato masher until it forms a thick purée. Leave to cool a little, then blend in the beaten eggs, cream, seasonings, nutmeg and orange zest.

Heat the oven to 180°C/350°F/gas mark 4. Turn the mixture into 6–8 buttered ramekins or a 1l/1¾pt buttered soufflé dish and place in a roasting pan. Add water to come two-thirds of the way up the ramekins or soufflé dish and put in the oven. Bake until firm, about 25 minutes for the ramekins and at least 35-40 minutes for the soufflé dish.

To serve, run a knife blade around the inside of the ramekins to loosen the mixture and turn out the custards on to plates. If you have used the soufflé dish, you can serve the custard in it.

# TOURTE DE LA VALLEE DE MUNSTER

## *Pork Plate Pie with Puff Pastry*

*A large slab of this type of* tourte *is offered as part of the* repas marcaire *(see page 107).*

**SERVES 8**
**FOR THE PASTRY**
**200g/7oz plain flour**
**50g/2oz salted butter**
**50g/2oz margarine**
**pinch of salt**

**100g/3 ½ oz stale bread, cut in cubes**
**milk, for soaking bread**
**1.2kg/2 ½ lb boneless pork shoulder,**
**trimmed and roughly chopped**
**pinch of nutmeg**
**plenty of chopped parsley**
**1 onion, finely chopped**
**2 eggs**
**300g/10oz bought puff pastry**
**salt and freshly ground black pepper**

To make the pastry, sift the flour into a mixing bowl or the goblet of a food processor. Cut the butter and margarine into small pieces, add them to the bowl and blend until the mixture resembles fine crumbs. Add 7 teaspoons of iced water and process to a dough. Wrap the pastry in cling film and refrigerate while you make the filling.

Soak the bread in some milk for at least 30 minutes or until soft. Chop the meat coarsely in the food processor (in several batches if necessary) with salt, pepper, nutmeg and parsley. Squeeze out the excess milk from the bread and add the bread, onion and one of the eggs to the meat in the food processor. Process until thoroughly mixed.

Grease a 30cm/12in loose-bottomed quiche tin. Roll out the shortcrust pastry to a circle rather larger than the tin. Lay it in the tin and trim the edge of the pastry with scissors, leaving an overhang of about 3cm/1 ¼ in. With wet hands, lift the meat mixture out of the processor and mound it up on the pastry. Turn the overhanging pastry in over the meat and brush it with water. Roll out the puff pastry to a circle that just fits the tin. Lay it on top of the meat and pastry, pressing it against the shortcrust pastry to seal. Cross-hatch the top decoratively with the point of a knife.

Preheat the oven to 220˚C/425˚F/gas mark 7. Beat the remaining egg and brush the pastry with it. To ensure that the bottom pastry is cooked, bake the *tourte* on a rack placed on the bottom of the oven for 15-20 minutes, then reduce the heat to 180˚C/350˚F/gas mark 4 and raise the *tourte* to the middle part of the oven. Continue baking for a further 40-45 minutes or until the filling is thoroughly hot (test with a skewer inserted into the middle) and the pastry is a rich golden brown. Serve warm.

# PATE VOSGIEN

## *Pork, Veal and Sausagemeat Free-formed Pie*

*The recipe for this excellent rectangular meat pie comes from Monsieur Jacquat, the butcher in Munster. When asked how many people the recipe served, his response was: 'six alsaciens or eight petits Parisiens'. On a picnic in the Vosges, seven Brits demolished it without much bother. (Illustrated opposite)*

**SERVES 6-8**
**700g/1 ½ lb boneless pork shoulder**
**300g/10oz boneless veal shoulder**

**plenty of chopped parsley**
**2 shallots, finely chopped**
**wine glass of dry white wine**
**250g/9oz finely ground pork sausagemeat**
**300g/10oz bought puff pastry**
**1 egg yolk, beaten**
**salt and freshly ground black pepper**

**FOR THE PASTRY**
**200g/7oz plain flour**
**50g/2oz salted butter**
**50g/2oz margarine**
**pinch of salt**

meats, beating well to blend and lighten the mixture. Roll out the shortcrust pastry to a rectangle 30 x 20cm/12 x 8in. Put it on a baking sheet with a lip, lined with non-stick baking paper. Arrange the meat on the pastry leaving a 4cm/1 ½ in border all around. Turn the border up over the meat. Roll out the puff pastry and cut a rectangle that will just fit the meat and pastry. Brush the exposed edge of shortcrust with water and lay the puff pastry on top. Press the edges together to seal. Preheat the oven to 200°C/400°F/gas mark 6. Decorate with a lattice or leaves made from the puff pastry trimmings, then brush with the beaten egg yolk.

Bake the pie in the lower part of the oven for 20 minutes or until the pastry is a good golden brown. Lower the heat to 180°C/350°F/gas mark 4, raise the pie to the middle part of the oven and bake for a further 30-40 minutes. To check it is cooked, insert a skewer into the fattest point – it should feel uncomfortably warm to the back of the hand. Cool on a rack.

# LAPIN GRAND'MERE

### Granny's Rabbit Stew in Wine Sauce

*This excellent rabbit dish comes from Madame Marck, a wonderful cook in Lautenbach-Zell in the Florival. The rabbit pieces are first marinated in a bottle of wine (half red, half white) for a tasty dish. She serves it with* Spätzle *(see page 41) or* Pâtes Maison *(see page 73).*

**SERVES 4-6**
**FOR THE MARINADE**
**½ bottle red wine**
**½ bottle white wine**
**bay leaf**
**several sprigs of parsley**
**2 cloves**
**nutmeg**
**1 garlic clove, sliced**
**1 onion, chopped**
**1 small leek, sliced**
**piece of celeriac or 1 stick celery,**
**finely diced**
**1 carrot, finely diced**
**salt and freshly ground black pepper**

**FOR THE STEW**
**young rabbit about 1.5kg/3 ½ lb**
**2-3tbsp oil**
**50g/2oz unsalted butter**
**seasoned flour, for coating**
**250-300ml/8-10fl oz stock**

Begin preparing this dish a day in advance. Put the marinade ingredients in a shallow, non-metallic bowl and mix together. Cut the rabbit into 10 pieces, or ask the butcher to do this, and add to the marinade. Cover with cling film and leave to marinate for 12-24 hours in the refrigerator, turning once or twice.

Using a slotted spoon, lift the rabbit pieces out of the marinade and pat dry on paper towels. Toss them in seasoned flour. Heat the oil in a large frying pan and cook until lightly golden on all sides. Transfer the pieces as they are ready to a large casserole, then clean out the frying pan. Lift out and drain the marinade vegetables, reserving the marinade in a saucepan. Melt the butter in the frying pan, soften the vegetables in it, then add them to the casserole. Bring the marinade to the boil and skim off any scum that rises. Pour the marinade into the casserole and add enough stock to barely cover the rabbit. Put on the lid and simmer very gently for about 45 minutes or until tender.

Start making this dish at least one, if not two days beforehand. Cut the pork and veal into pieces the size of your middle finger. Put in a non-metallic bowl with the parsley, shallots, seasoning and wine. Mix well. Cover and leave to marinate in a cool place for 24–48 hours.

Make up the pastry with the flour, salt, butter, margarine and cold water according to your preferred pastry recipe, or as instructed on page 124. Wrap the pastry in cling film and refrigerate.

Remove the meat with a slotted spoon and place in a basin. Mix the sausagemeat into the

# FILETS DE CHEVREUIL AUX CHAMPIGNONS EN CROUTE

### Fillets of Venison with Mushrooms En Croûte

*Although this recipe is complicated and extravagant, it is worth the work and expense for a special splash. Providing the prepared stuffing and meat are well chilled, the assembled dish will keep for 24 hours in the refrigerator ready for baking, making it ideal for dinner parties. Accompany with robust, seasonal vegetables such as* Chou Rouge à l'Alsacienne *(see page 122) or* Flans de Potiron *(see page 122).*

**SERVES 6**

**1.35kg/3lb saddle of venison (preferably roe deer)**

**FOR THE STOCK**

**2 carrots, roughly chopped**
**2 onions, halved, skins left on**
**2tbsp oil**
**250ml/8fl oz red wine**
**few parsley stalks**
**few thyme sprigs**
**2 bay leaves**

**FOR THE STUFFING**

**1 shallot, finely chopped**
**25g/1oz butter**
**150g/5oz cultivated or wild mushrooms, finely chopped**
**salt and freshly ground black pepper**
**1 egg, separated**
**100ml/3½fl oz crème fraîche**
**pinch of nutmeg**
**oil, for searing**
**400g/14oz bought puff pastry**

**FOR THE SAUCE**

**2tbsp redcurrant jelly**
**50-100g/2-3½oz unsalted butter, cut in pieces**

Preheat the oven to 220°C/425°F/gas mark 7. Bone the saddle, or ask the butcher to do this for you, to give two fillets weighing about 350g/12oz each, two little undercuts and some trimmings. Reserve the bones. Divest the fillets of any membrane or tendons.

To make the stock, chop the bones up roughly and roast them for about 20 minutes in the hot oven with the carrots, onions and oil until well browned. Scrape them into a large saucepan or flameproof casserole, add the wine and enough water to cover the bones, the parsley stalks, thyme sprigs and bay leaves. Bring to the boil and simmer for 1-2 hours. Strain the stock and chill it. Degrease the stock, return it to the saucepan and reduce it by fast boiling to about 1 cupful. Reserve for the redcurrant sauce.

To make the stuffing, heat the butter in a saucepan and soften the shallot. Add the mushrooms, salt and pepper. Cover and cook gently to render the juices. Uncover and raise the heat to evaporate the juices. Scrape the mushrooms into a bowl and leave to cool. Roughly chop the venison undercuts and trimmings and put in the food processor with the mushrooms, egg white, crème fraîche and nutmeg. Season to taste. Process to a fairly coarse sausagemeat consistency.

Dry the fillets and sear them briefly on all sides in hot oil. Cool them on a rack. Meanwhile, roll out the pastry to a large rectangle a little wider than one fillet and long enough to fold over to enclose it generously. Place it on a baking sheet lined with non-stick baking paper. Sandwich the two fillets together with the mushroom stuffing and put

them at one end of the pastry. Brush around the edges with water and bring the pastry up and over to enclose. With scissors, cut away one layer of pastry at the ends where it is double thick, and fold the single layer under. Use any trimmings to make decorations. Brush with beaten egg yolk. Chill until baking time.

Preheat the oven to 220°C/425°F/ gas mark 7. Bake the venison at the bottom of the oven, to ensure the pastry underneath is cooked: 25-30 minutes for rare, 30-35 minutes for medium or 40 minutes for well done.

Meanwhile make the sauce. Reheat the reserved stock. Whisk in the redcurrant jelly and, off the heat, the butter one piece at a time. Check the seasoning.

# PAIN AUX NOIX ET AUX LARDONS

### Wholewheat Walnut and Bacon Loaf

*This magnificent loaf, slow to stale, keeps excellent company with a well-aged Munster or a robust bowl of soup for supper.*

**MAKES 1 LOAF**

**300g/10oz wholewheat flour**
**200g/7oz strong white bread flour**
**1tsp salt**
**15g/½oz fresh yeast or 1 pkt easy-blend dry yeast (6g/¼oz )**
**1tbsp oil**
**100g/3½oz lardons**
**100g/3½oz walnuts, roughly chopped**

If you have a heavy-duty mixer with a dough hook, use it to make the dough. Otherwise use a large bowl to mix the dough, and knead by hand. Mix together the flours and salt.

Crumble or sprinkle the yeast over the flour. Mix the oil with 300ml/10fl oz of warm water and add to the bowl. Work up to a firm dough that does not stick excessively to the bowl or to your hands, adding more flour if necessary. Encase the whole bowl in a large plastic bag and leave the dough to rise until doubled in bulk – about 2 hours at room temperature.

Fry the lardons very gently until the fat renders and then drain them. Do not let them get too brown or they will harden in the bread. Turn out the dough onto a floured surface and knock it back. Knead in the lardons and walnuts. Turn into a 6cm/2½in deep, lightly oiled 25 x 10cm/10 x 4in loaf tin and leave to rise to the top of the tin. Preheat the oven to 220°C/425°F/gas mark 7. Bake the loaf for

10-15 minutes, then reduce the temperature to 200°C/400°/gas mark 6 and bake for a further 25-30 minutes or until golden brown and hollow-sounding when tapped on the bottom.

# GLACE AU MIEL DE SAPIN AUX FRUITS DES BOIS

*Pine Honey Ice Cream with Fruits of the Forest*

*This recipe celebrates all the fragrance of the Vosges. The ice cream could not be quicker to make. (Illustrated above)*

**SERVES 4-6**
**3 egg yolks**
**1 egg**
**175g/6oz *miel de sapin* (dark honeydew honey)**
**300ml/10fl oz whipping cream**
**mixed raspberries, blackberries, bilberries and cranberries, to serve**

With an electric mixer, beat together the yolks, egg and honey until thoroughly fluffy and tripled in bulk. Whip the cream to soft peaks and gently fold it in to the egg and honey mixure with a metal spoon. Freeze in small containers such as yogurt pots or ramekins. To serve, turn out and surround with fruit. Eat within 2-3 days.

# TARTE AUX MYRTILLES SAUVAGES

## Wild Bilberry Tart

*There are many versions of bilberry tart, but Monsieur Gilg's is one of the best. For notes on baking tarts and quiches see* Tarte à l'Oignon, *page 69. (Illustrated opposite)*

**SERVES 6-8 PEOPLE**
**FOR THE SWEET SHORTCRUST PASTRY**
**250g/9oz plain flour**
**125g/4 ½ oz unsalted butter**
**3tbsp caster sugar**
**pinch of salt**
**1 egg yolk**

**FOR THE FILLING**
**at least 1kg/2 ¼ lb fresh wild bilberries, or frozen, thawed and well-drained**
**2 eggs**
**60g/2 ½ oz caster sugar**
**2tbsp plain flour**
**150ml/5fl oz crème fraîche**
**icing sugar, to finish**

To make the pastry sift the flour into a mixing bowl and make a large well in the centre. Using your finger tips, work the butter, sugar, salt, egg yolk and 2 tablespoons of cold water into the flour until absorbed. Cover with cling film and refrigerate for at least 30 minutes.

Preheat the oven to 200°C/400°F/gas mark 6. Roll out the pastry quite thickly and use it to line a lightly buttered 30cm/12in loose-bottomed quiche tin. Pick over the bilberries but do not wash them or they will exude too much juice in the cooking. Fill the pastry with them and bake the tart either on the bottom of the oven or on a preheated black baking sheet placed on an oven shelf for 20 minutes.

Whisk together the eggs, sugar, flour and crème fraîche. Remove the tart from the oven and use a tablespoon, ladle or paper towels to remove any excess juice floating on top of the fruit (there will be lots if you have used frozen fruit). Pour over the egg mixture and smooth with the back of a spoon. Reduce the temperature to 180°C/350°F/gas mark 4 and bake the tart in the middle of the oven for 20 minutes or until set and the pastry is golden.

Allow to cool in the tin, then unmould and sprinkle with icing sugar to serve.

# MOUSSE AU FROMAGE BLANC, COULIS DE FRAMBOISES

## Fromage Blanc *Mousse with Raspberry Coulis*

*This beautifully light, white dessert makes a perfect end to a rich meal.*

**SERVES 6**
**4 gelatine sheets or 1tbsp powdered gelatine**
**50g/2oz caster sugar**
**250ml/8fl oz full-fat *fromage blanc* (40% fat content) or Greek yogurt**
**zest of 1 lemon, grated**
**250ml/8fl oz whipping cream**

**FOR THE COULIS**
**500g/18oz raspberries or other soft fruit**
**sugar, to taste**
**mint leaves, to garnish**

Soak the gelatine sheets in copious cold water until floppy, then squeeze out, or sprinkle the powdered gelatine over 2 tablespoons of water and leave till spongy. Dissolve the sugar in 2 tablespoons of water, add the gelatine sheets or the sponged gelatine and stir over gentle heat until dissolved. Whisk the dissolved gelatine into the *fromage blanc* with the lemon zest. Whip the cream until it holds its shape and fold it in to the mixture. Turn the mixture into a lightly oiled 24cm/9 ½ in cake tin, or mould in 6 yoghurt pots.

To make the coulis, liquidize the fruit with sugar to taste, then push through a sieve to remove the seeds and pips.

To serve the mousse, turn out over a pool of coulis and garnish with mint leaves.

# PARFAIT GLACE AU KIRSCH

## Frozen Kirsch Parfait

**SERVES 6-8**
**4 eggs, separated**
**100g/3 ½ oz caster sugar**
**2 pinches powdered vanilla or 1tsp vanilla extract**
**200ml/7fl oz whipping cream**
**4tbsp Kirsch**
**sour cherries in Kirsch (*griottes au Kirsch*), to serve**

Beat the egg yolks with half of the sugar and the vanilla until thoroughly light and fluffy. Whip the cream to stiff peaks and add the Kirsch. Beat the egg whites to soft peaks, add the rest of the sugar and continue beating until stiff but still creamy and supple. Fold the three preparations together and tip either into a 7cm/3in deep, 30 x 10cm/12 x 4in loaf tin or a serving bowl or individual coupes. Cover and freeze for several hours or until firm. Eat the ice cream within 2-3 days, adding *griottes au Kirsch* to serve.

# A VISITOR'S GUIDE

Some of the eating places mentioned here feature in the text, others were beyond the scope of the book but are included for extra information and handy reference. The restaurants are chosen for their food, sympathetic atmosphere and general typicity, and range from the humblest *ferme-auberge* to the grandest restaurant. Michelin-starred establishments are indicated (*), otherwise there is no attempt at rating and the list is entirely subjective. *Fermes-auberges* and *tables d'hôtes* establishments are often open only at weekends, some only during the summer months. A *fermes-auberges* guide (FF53) is published by the Association des Fermes-Auberges du Haut-Rhin, BP 371, Colmar, Tel 89 20 10 68. They also publish a *Guide des Gites Ruraux du Haut-Rhin* (FF35)

and a *Guide des Chambres d'Hôte* (FF20). All are available at Tourist Offices and Syndicats d'Initiative.

Places of interest and specialities listed here embrace a broad range of things related to the art and culture of the table: food and wine-oriented museums, exhibitions and herb gardens, as well as glass, tableware and table linen manufacturers and *charcuterie*, cheese and wine producers. Some of these last will despatch produce by mail. Many a homesick *alsacien* exiled from Alsace sends off at Christmas for his *Bredle* (Christmas biscuits), hams, sausages, foie gras, *vins d'Alsace*, *eaux-de-vie* and other typically Alsatian delicacies.

There is nothing the *alsaciens* love more than a village or street party. These happen throughout the year,

especially in summer and autumn. Variously called *fête*, *foire*, *messti* or *kermesse*, they may be simply the village's annual 'knees-up' (*foire* or *fête communale or du village*), or they may be devoted to some speciality (*fête de la cerise, de la tourte, de la biére* or – plenty of these – *fête du vin*). The streets sprout trestle tables and benches, the wine and beer begins to flow, oom-pa-pa music blares out and the village gets partying. They are a wonderful feature of Alsace life and should on no account be missed. It is impossible to list them all; the ones mentioned are the best known or my personal favourites. A comprehensive, tri-lingual (French/German/English) calendar entitled Manifestations/Veranstaltungen/Events is produced by the Tourist Office.

Some useful addresses:

OFFICE DEPARTEMENTAL DU TOURISME DU BAS-RHIN
9 rue du Dôme,
Strasbourg
Tel 88 32 17 77

ASSOCIATION DEPARTAMENTALE DU TOURISME DU HAUT-RHIN
Maison du Tourisme,
1 rue Schlumberger,
Colmar
Tel 89 20 10 68

MAISON DE L'ALSACE
39 Avenue des Champs Elysées,
Paris
Tel (1) 42 56 15 94

## NORTHERN ALSACE

**Restaurants, Winstubs and Fermes-Auberges**

S'BURJERSTUEWEL
(chez Yvonne)
10 rue du Sanglier,
Strasbourg
Tel 88 88 32 84 15

S'MUNSTERSTUEWEL
8 place du Marché-aux-Cochons-de-Lait,
Strasbourg
Tel 88 32 17 63

MAISON KAMMERZELL
16 place de la Cathédrale,
Strasbourg
Tel 88 32 42 14

LE CROCODILE (***)
10 rue de l'Outre,
Strasbourg
Tel 88 32 23 02

LE BUEREHIESEL (***)
4 parc de l'Orangerie, Strasbourg
Tel 88 61 62 24

A LA CHARRUE
30 rue de la République,
Hoerdt
Tel 88 51 31 11

AUBERGE DU CHEVAL BLANC (**)
4 route de Wissembourg, Lembach
Tel 88 94 41 86

FERME-AUBERGE DU MOULIN DES SEPT FONTAINES
Drachenbronn
Tel 88 94 50 90

S'BATSBERGER STULWEL
25 rue Principale, Imbsheim
Tel 88 70 73 85

ENS NEUBURS
16 rue Principale,
Buswiller
Tel 88 70 97 54

HOSTELLERIE DU CERF (**)
30 rue du Général de Gaulle,
Marlenheim
Tel 88 87 73 73

CHEZ PHILIPPE
4 place de l'Eglise, Blaesheim
Tel 88 68 86 00

**Places of interest**

CHRISTIANE BISCH
(cookery school)
22 rue Baldner,
Strasbourg-Neudorf
Tel 88 44 29 23 or 88 79 04 03

MUSEE DES ARTS DECORATIFS
(in the Palais Rohan)
(porcelain)
place du Château, Strasbourg
Tel 88 52 50 00

MUSEE ALSACIEN
(popular arts and crafts)
23 quai Saint-Nicolas,
Strasbourg
Tel 88 35 55 36

MUSEE DE L'OEUVRE NOTRE-DAME
(Medieval and Renaissance art,
herb garden)
place du Château, Strasbourg
Tel 88 32 88 17

MUSEE DU PAYS DE HANAU
(local costumes, arts and crafts)
place du Château,
Bouxwiller
Tel 88 70 70 16

MUSEE DES ARTS ET TRADITIONS
POPULAIRES
(Christmas biscuit mould collection)
rue des Remparts,
La Petite Pierre
Tel 88 70 41 41

LA MAISON DU VERRE ET DU
CRISTAL
(history of glass-making)
Meisenthal
Tel 87 96 91 51

VERRERIES ROYALES DE SAINT
LOUIS
(glass factory and shop)
Saint-Louis-le-Bitche, Lemberg
Tel 87 06 40 04

MAISON DU KOCHERSBERG
(exhibitions of Kochersberg traditions)
place du Marché,
Truchtersheim
Tel (Mairie) 88 69 60 30

**Specialities of the region**

FRICK-LUTZ
(meat, *charcuterie*)
16 rue des Orfevres,
Strasbourg
Tel 88 32 60 60

CCA-LA CHARCUTERIE ALSACIENNE
(meat, *charcuterie*)
39 rue du 22 Novembre,
Strasbourg
Tel 88 75 16 04

JEAN LUTZ
(foie gras)
5 rue de Chaudron, Strasbourg
Tel 88 32 00 64

BURGARD
(*bretzels*)
22 rue des Orfevres, Strasbourg
Tel 88 22 67 30

*TOP Steeply roofed, half-timbered
houses beside the river Ill in the
Petite France quarter of Strasbourg.
ABOVE AND LEFT The lovely old
pedestrian quarter of Strasbourg in
the heart of the city is famous for its
Winstubs or wine bars, where
simple local dishes are served with
jugs of wine.*

ABOVE *Bouxwiller town houses all dressed up for Christmas.*
BELOW *La Petite Pierre.*
OPPOSITE RIGHT *Local dancers at St Hippolyte.*
OPPOSITE LEFT *The town of Keintzheim.*

NAEGEL
(*pâtisserie, traiteur*)
9 rue des Orfèvres,
Strasbourg
Tel 88 32 82 86

CHRISTIAN
(*pâtisserie*, chocolate, tea room)
18 rue Mercière
and 12 rue de l'Outre,
Strasbourg
Tel 88 22 12 70 and 88 32 04 41

MULHAUPT
(*pâtisserie*)
18 rue du Vieux-Marché-aux-Poissons,
Strasbourg
Tel 88 23 15 02

SCHOLLER
(organic and sourdough breads)
10 place Broglie, Strasbourg
Tel 88 32 39 09

WOERLE
(bread)
10 rue de la Division-Leclerc,
Strasbourg
Tel 88 32 00 88

GERARD BLONDEAU-LA FROMAGERE
(cheese)
13 route de Saverne, Oberhausbergen
(and markets: boulevard de la Marne,
Tues/Sat; place Broglie, Wed/Fri)
Tel 88 56 20 79

EMILE HEIL
(*pain paysan*)
15 rue des Vosges, Wingen
Tel 88 94 40 10

ALBERT GRAMMES
(goats' cheese)
24 route de Mattstall, Lembach
Tel 88 94 21 72

CAVE VINICOLE DE CLEEBOURG
(wine)
route du Vin, Cleebourg
Tel 88 94 50 33

BOUCHERIE-CHARCUTERIE
RICHERT
(*charcuterie*, game), Lembach
Tel 88 94 40 14

PATISSERIE-CONFISERIE ISENMANN
(*pâtisserie*, Christmas biscuits)
28 Grand-Rue, Bouxwiller
Tel 88 70 70 50

BOUCHERIE-CHARCUTERIE
MARIUS
(*charcuterie, tourtes*)
50 Grand-Rue,
Bouxwiller
Tel 88 70 71 04

BRASSERIE METEOR
(beer)
Hochfelden
Tel 88 71 73 73

**Markets**

Tuesday: *Hochfelden, Strasbourg*
(Neudorf, boulevard de la Marne and
place de Bordeaux)
Wednesday: *Brumath*
Friday: *Strasbourg* (place Broglie)
Saturday: *Marlenheim, Barr,
Wissembourg, Strasbourg* (Neudorf,
boulevard de la Marne, place de
Bordeaux and place du Marché-aux-
Poissons)

**Fairs and festivals**

May: *Fête des asperges* (asparagus
festival) Hoerdt
end September: *Foire aux Oignons*
(onion fair), Brumath
last Sunday in September: *Fête des
Vendanges* (wine harvest festival),
Cleebourg
end September/early October: *Fête de
la Choucroute* (Sauerkraut festival),
Krautergersheim
fourth Sunday in November until
Christmas Eve: *Christkindelsmarik*
(Christmas market), Strasbourg
December: *Foire de Noël* (Christmas
market), Bouxwiller

## THE ROUTE DES VINS

**Restaurants, Winstubs, *Caveaux***

HOSTELLERIE DU CERF (**)
30 rue Gral. de Gaulle,
Marlenheim
Tel 88 87 73 73

CAVEAU NARTZ
Dambach-la-Ville
Tel 88 92 41 11

WISTUB DU SOMMELIER
51 Grand'rue,
Bergheim
Tel 89 73 69 99

WISTUB ZUM PFIFFERHUS
14 Grand'rue, Ribeauvillé
Tel 89 73 62 28

AUX ARMES DE FRANCE (*)
1 Grand'rue,
Ammerschwihr
Tel 89 47 10 12

AU FER ROUGE (*)
52 Grand'rue, Colmar
Tel 89 41 37 24

MAISON DES TETES
19 rue des Têtes, Colmar
Tel 89 24 43 43

AUX TROIS POISSONS
15 quai de la Poissonerie,
Colmar
Tel 89 41 25 21

WISTUB BRENNER
1 rue Turenne, Colmar
Tel 89 41 42 33

CAVEAU SAINT JEAN
47 Grand'rue, Colmar
Tel 89 41 68 02

AUBERGE DU VEILLEUR
12 place Turenne, Turckheim
Tel 89 27 32 22

LE PAVILLON GOURMAND
101 rue du Rempart-Sud,
Eguisheim
Tel 89 24 36 88

LA GRANGELIERE
59 rue du Rempart-Sud,
Eguisheim
Tel 89 23 00 30

**Places of interest**

MUSEE DE LA FOLIE MARCO
(eighteenth-century house and
garden)
Barr
Tel 88 08 66 65

MUSEE D'UNTERLINDEN
(medieval to modern art, wine
artefacts)
1 rue des Unterlinden,
Colmar
Tel 89 41 89 23

CONFRERIE DE ST ETIENNE and
MUSEE DU VIGNOBLE ET DES VINS
D'ALSACE
(wine *confrérie*, wine collection and
museum)
Château de Kientzheim,
Kientzheim
Tel 89 78 23 84 (*Confrérie*); 89 78 21
36 (*Musée*)

COMITE D'EXPLOITATION DU
TRAIN FOLKLORIQUE DE
ROSHEIM-OTTROTT
(steam train from Rosheim to Ottrott)
Ottrott
Tel 88 95 91 14

**Specialities of the region**

SIFFERT
(cheese)
35 route de Rosenwiller,
Rosheim
Tel 88 50 20 13

*RIGHT A grape picker at work near Wangen in northern Alsace. In former times, growers here were levied part of their wine by the lord of the manor each year. Nowadays, in July the suppression of this hated tax is commemorated in a joyous festival where wine flows freely.*

*ABOVE The ruins of the medieval château of St Ulrich tower over the picturesque wine-growing town of Ribeauvillé. Some of the finest Rieslings in Alsace are grown in the vineyards that line the steep slopes above the town.*
*LEFT The classic Kougelhopf mould adorns this baker's shop front. This light, cake-like sweet loaf is typical of the area.*
*OPPOSITE Intricate shop signs in Eguisheim and Riquewhir.*

CHRISTINE FERBER
(jams)
18 rue des Trois-Epis,
Niedermorschwihr
Tel 89 27 05 69

LA FROMAGERIE SAINT-NICOLAS
(cheese)
18 rue Saint-Nicolas, Colmar
Tel 89 24 90 45

MAISON PFISTER
(wine, *eaux-de-vie*)
11 rue des Marchands, Colmar
Tel 89 41 33 61

LEONARD HELMSTETTER
(bread)
11-13 rue des Serruriers, Colmar
Tel 89 41 27 78

GLASSER
(*charcuterie*, pies)
18 rue des Boulangers, Colmar
Tel 89 41 23 69

JEAN
(chocolate, *pâtisserie*)
6 place de l'Ecole, Colmar
Tel 89 41 24 63

POISSONERIE WERTZ
(fish)
20 quai de la Poissonnerie,
Colmar
Tel 89 24 32 92

LA COTONNIERE D'ALSACE (PAULE MARROT)
(tablecloths, furnishing fabrics)
1 rue des Clefs, Colmar
Tel 89 22 46 00

ARTS ET COLLECTIONS D'ALSACE
(gifts and collectibles)
1 place de l'Ancienne Douane,
Colmar
Tel 89 24 09 78

GRIMMER
(chocolate)
61 route de Colmar,
Wintzenheim
Tel 89 80 60 40

GILBERT MARX
(bread, *bretzels*)
39 Grand'rue, Eguisheim
Tel 89 41 32 56

GILBERT SCHLURAFF
(meat)
69 rue Maréchal de Lattre de Tassigny,
Soultz
Tel 89 76 95 62

A. SCHELLENBERGER
(organic and other meat)
1 rue Maréchal de Lattre de Tassigny,
Soultz
Tel 89 76 85 06

**Wine growers**

ROMAIN FRITSCH
49 rue Gral. de Gaulle, Marlenheim
Tel 88 87 51 23

FREDERIC MOCHEL
56 rue Principale, Traenheim
Tel 88 50 38 67

ROLAND SCHMITT
35 rue des Vosges, Bergbieten
Tel 88 38 20 72

JEAN HEYWANG
7 rue Principale, Heiligenstein
Tel 88 08 91 41

ALBERT SELTZ
21 rue Principale,
Mittelbergheim
Tel 88 08 91 77

ARMAND GILG
2 rue Rotland, Mittelbergheim
Tel 88 08 92 76

MARC KREYDENWEISS
12 rue Deharbe, Andlau
Tel 88 08 95 83

J. L. DIRRINGER
5 rue Maréchal Foch,
Dambach-la-Ville
Tel 88 92 41 51

ROLLY-GASSMANN
1 rue de l'Eglise, Rorschwihr
Tel 89 73 63 28

MARCEL DEISS ET FILS
15 route du Vin, Bergheim
Tel 89 73 63 37

ANDRE KIENTZLER
50 route de Bergheim, Ribeauvillé
Tel 89 73 67 10

HUGEL ET FILS
3 rue de la 1ère Armée,
Riquewihr
Tel 89 47 92 15

FREDERIC MALLO
2 rue St Jacques, Hunawihr
Tel 89 73 61 41

CAVES J. B. ADAM
6 rue de l'Aigle,
Ammerschwihr
Tel 89 78 23 21

CAVE VINICOLE DE TURCKHEIM
16 rue des Tuileries,
Turckheim
Tel 89 27 06 25

DOMAINE ZIND-HUMBRECHT
route de Colmar,
Turckheim
Tel 89 27 02 05

LEON BEYER
2 rue de la 1ère Armée Française,
Eguisheim
Tel 89 41 41 05

KUENTZ-BAS
14 route du Vin,
Husseren-les-Chateaux
Tel 89 49 30 24

THEO CATTIN
35 rue Roger Frémeaux,
Voegtlinshoffen
Tel 89 49 30 43

DOMAINE LUCIEN ALBRECHT
9 Grand'rue, Orschwihr
Tel 89 76 95 18

DIRLER
13 rue d'Issenheim, Bergholtz
Tel 89 76 91 00

DOMAINES SCHLUMBERGER
100 rue Théodore Deck,
Guebwiller
Tel 89 74 27 00

## Markets

Monday: *Kaysersberg, Bergheim*
Wednesday: *Andlau, Dambach-la-Ville, Rouffach* (5-7 p.m. organic produce)
Thursday: *Obernai, Colmar*
Friday: *Rosheim, Turckheim, Wintzenheim, Riquewihr*
Saturday: *Barr, Colmar, Rouffach, Ribeauvillé, Thann*

## Fairs and festivals

last Sunday in April: *Foire aux Vins* (wine fair) Ammerschwihr
around May Day: *Fête de l'Escargot* (snail festival) Osenbach
Ascension weekend: *Foire du Vin, Pain et Fromage Eco-biologiques* (organic and bio-dynamic wine, bread and cheese fair) Rouffach
first fortnight in June: *Fête du Kougelhopf* (Kougelhopf festival) Ribeauvillé
second and third Sundays in June: *Fête de la Cerise* (cherry fair) Westhoffen
first Saturday in July: *Nuit du Vin* (evening wine festival) Dambach-la-Ville
last weekend in July: *Fête du Vin* (wine festival) Mittelbergheim
Sunday before 15 August: *Fête du Klevener* (fair celebrating local white wine) Heiligenstein
14-15 August: *Mariage de l'Ami Fritz* (traditional pageant) Marlenheim
mid-August: *Fête de l'Amitié 'Portes et Caves ouvertes'* (wine and art fair) Gueberschwihr
third Sunday in August: *Fête du*

*Village et du Rouge d'Ottrott* (fair celebrating local red wine) Ottrott
first Sunday in September: *Pfifferdäj* (pipers' day) Ribeauvillé
first Sunday in October: *Fête des Vendanges* (grape picking festival) Barr
second Sunday in October: *Fête du Vin Nouveau* (new wine festival) Itterswiller
three weekends preceding Christmas: *Noêl à Kaysersberg* (Christmas market) Kaysersberg

# THE SUNDGAU

**Restaurants, Brasseries,**
*Fermes-Auberges*

BRASSERIE GAMBRINUS
5 rue des Franciscains,
Mulhouse
Tel 89 66 18 65

HOTEL DU PARC
26 rue de la Sinne,
Mulhouse
Tel 89 66 12 22

LE PETIT ZINC
15 rue des Bons-Enfants,
Mulhouse
Tel 89 46 36 78

LA POSTE (*)
7 rue du Gral. de Gaulle,
Riedesheim
Tel 89 44 07 71

LA TONNELLE (*)
61 rue du Maréchal-Joffre,
Riedesheim
Tel 89 54 25 77

RESTAURANT AU SOLEIL
17 Grand'rue,
Ueberstrass
Tel 89 25 60 13

LA MARMITE
39 rue du 1er Septembre,
Muespach
Tel 89 68 62 62

AUBERGE ET HOSTELLERIE
PAYSANNE
24 rue de Wolschwiller, Lutter
Tel 89 40 71 67

AUBERGE DU VIEUX MOULIN DE
BENDORF
route de Winkel, Bendorf
Tel 89 40 81 38

AUBERGE DU MORIMONT
Ferme Morimont, Oberlarg
Tel 89 40 88 92

HOTEL-RESTAURANT DU PETIT
KOHLBERG
Petit Kohlberg
Tel 89 40 85 30

AUBERGE ST BRICE
Chapelle de St Brice,
Oltingue
Tel 89 40 74 31

CAFE-RESTAURANT AU CHEVAL
BLANC
20 rue Principale, Kiffis,
Tel 89 40 33 05

HOTEL-RESTAURANT JENNY
84 rue de Hégenheim,
Hagenthal-le-Bas
Tel 89 68 50 09

RESTAURANT LA COURONNE
6 rue du Soleil, Buschwiller
Tel 89 69 12 62

RESTAURANT L'ANCIENNE FORGE
52 rue Principale,
Hagenthal-le-Haut
Tel 89 68 56 10

RESTAURANT BIRY
5 rue de Belfort,
Village-Neuf
Tel 89 69 17 60

**Places of interest**

MUSEE FRANCAIS DU
CHEMIN DE FER
(trains)
3 Alfred de Glehn,
Mulhouse
Tel 89 42 25 67

MUSEE DE L'AUTOMOBILE
(Schlumpf veteran car
collection)
192 avenue de Colmar,
Mulhouse
Tel 89 42 29 17

MUSEE DE L'IMPRESSION
SUR ETOFFES
(textile printing)
3 rue des Bonnes-Gens,
Mulhouse
Tel 89 45 51 20

MUSEE HISTORIQUE
Hôtel de Ville,
Mulhouse
Tel 89 45 43 20

ECOMUSEE D'ALSACE
(outdoor village-museum, timbered
houses, craft activities)
Ungersheim
Tel 89 74 44 74

MUSEE PAYSAN (MAISON DU
SUNDGAU)
(local costumes, artefacts)
Oltingue
Tel 89 40 79 24

## Specialities of the region

AU BOUTON D'OR
(cheese)
5 place de la Réunion,
Mulhouse
Tel 89 45 50 17

JACQUES
(*pâtisserie*, chocolates)
1 place de la Réunion, Mulhouse
Tel 89 66 45 46

CCA/LA CHARCUTERIE ALSACIENNE
(meat, *charcuterie*)
Cour des Maréchaux, Mulhouse
Tel 89 66 57 50

LES PETITES HALLES
(fruit, vegetables, herbs)
22 rue du Sauvage, Mulhouse
Tel 89 56 50 82

CAFES AU BON NEGRE
(coffee, tea)
22 rue du Sauvage, Mulhouse
Tel 89 45 15 13

BRETZELS ROLAND
(*bretzels*)
62 rue des Puits, Mulhouse
Tel 89 65 55 42

AU BRETZEL CHAUD
(*bretzels*)
41 rue du Sauvage, Mulhouse
Tel 89 46 65 22

COUVENT D'OELENBERG
(trappist cheese, vegetables, honey, flour)
rue Oelenberg, Reiningue
Tel 89 81 91 23

GISSINGER
(snail delicacies)
24 rue de l'Or, Hindlingen
Tel 89 25 70 62

SUNDGAU TERROIR
(local farm products)
50 rue de l'Eglise, Vieux-Ferrette
Tel 89 40 40 45

PAIN RUF
(sourdough and wholewheat breads
baked in wood-fired oven)
42 rue Principale,
Michelbach-le-Haut
Tel 89 68 75 01

SUNDGAUER KASKELLER
(cheese)
17 rue de la Montagne,
Vieux-Ferrette
Tel 89 40 42 22

ETIENNE FERNEX
(goats' cheese)
22 rue Principale, Biederthal
Tel 89 07 35 15

FERME WYSS-CHRISTEN
(goats' cheese)
15 Tannwald, Leymen
Tel 89 68 59 59

MOULIN DE HESINGUE
(wholewheat and baking flours)
3 rue du Moulin, Hésingue
Tel 89 69 18 23

FREUND ET FILS
(fine wines, Bordeaux, Burgundy)
1 rue de Bourgfelden, Hégenheim
Tel 89 69 09 09

GREDER FRERES
(wines, especially from
Eguisheim co-operative)
16 rue de Hésingue,
Hégenheim
Tel 89 69 17 97

ADRIEN VONARB
(Rhine fish and farmed trout, fish
dishes)
1 rue Mittelhardt,
Balgau
Tel 89 48 62 71 or 89 48 59 78

REMY MEYER
(Tomme des Prés du Ried cheese)
23 route de Sélestat,
Muttersholtz
Tel 88 85 12 42

MINOTERIE KIRCHER
(stoneground Maire, wholewheat, rye
and spelt flours)
Ebersheim
Tel 88 85 71 10

## Markets

Tuesday: *Mulhouse* (Canal Couvert)
Wednesday: *Riedesheim*
Thursday: *Mulhouse* (Canal Couvert)
Friday: *Waldighoffen*
Saturday: *Mulhouse* (Canal Couvert),
*Saint Louis, Altkirch*

## Fairs and festivals

third Thursday in April and
September: *Fête du Tissu* (furnishing
fabrics), Mulhouse
mid-May and mid-September:
*Sundgauer Büramart* (farmers'

market), Durmenach
last weekend in August: *Salon des
Vins et Fromages* (cheese and wine
fair), Hagenthal-le-Bas
second Sunday in September:
*Altbürafascht* (old-time farming
festival), Bernwiller
second Sunday in September:
*Fête du Pain* (bread), Michelbach-le-
Bas
first week in October: *Journées
d'Octobre* (autumn fair), Mulhouse
last Thursday in November: *Foire Ste
Catherine* (agricultural market),
Altkirch
early December: *Foire St Nicolas* (St
Nicholas fair), Ferrette

*ABOVE A carp pond in the
Sundgau. Ponds are freshly stocked
with carp each year during
March and April. Throughout the
summer months the fish are
fattened on a mixture of sweetcorn,
rye and barley, ready for the
fishing season in autumn.
OPPOSITE Bernwiller.*

## THE VOSGES

### Restaurants, *Fermes-Auberges*

AUBERGE DU SCHLUMPF
Dolleren
Tel 89 82 08 82

FERME-AUBERGE DU MOLKENRAIN
Wattwiller
Tel 89 81 17 66

TAVERNE DU VIGNERON
7 place St Léger,
Guebwiller
Tel 89 76 81 89

FERME-AUBERGE GLASHUTTE
Rimbach
Tel 89 76 88 04

FERME-AUBERGE BUCHWALD
Breitenbach
Tel 89 77 54 37

FERME-AUBERGE LAMEYSBERG
Breitenbach
Tel 89 77 35 30

FERME-AUBERGE CHRISTLESGUT
Breitenbach
Tel 89 77 51 11

FERME-AUBERGE KASTELBERG
route des Crétes,
Metzeral
Tel 89 77 62 25

FERME-AUBERGE DU HAYCOT
Le Bonhomme
Tel 89 47 21 46

FERME-AUBERGE DU PETIT-HAUT
Ste Marie-aux-Mines
Tel 89 58 72 15

FERME-AUBERGE DU GLASBORNLINGE
Orbey
Tel 89 77 37 78 or 89 77 59 35

FERME-AUBERGE KEBESPRE
Lapoutroie
Tel 89 47 50 71

FERME-AUBERGE IRRKRUT
Col de Fouchy
Tel 88 57 09 29

TABLE D'HOTE PROMONT
Ranrupt
Tel 88 97 62 85

LA PETITE AUBERGE
6 rue Principale,
Le Hohwald
Tel 88 08 33 05

### Places of interest

CHEMIN DE FER TOURISTIQUE DE
LA VALLEE DE LA DOLLER
(steam train Cernay-Sentheim )
10 rue de la Gare, Sentheim
Tel 89 82 88 48

LE MOULIN DE STORKENSOHN
(walnut mill)
Storkensohn
Tel 89 82 75 50

MUSEE DE LA SCHLITTE
(foresters' sledge museum)
Muhlbach
Tel 89 77 61 08

JARDIN D'ALTITUDE DU HAUT
CHITELET
(alpine plants in natural habitat)
Col de la Schlucht,
Gérardmer
Tel 29 63 31 46

MUSEE ET MEMORIAL DU LINGE
(First World War memorial and
museum)
Orbey

MAISON DU VAL DE VILLE
(traditions, handicrafts from
Val de Villé)
Albé
Tel 88 85 68 09

### Specialities of the region

BERNARD BRINGEL
(foie gras, *charcuterie*)
Guewenheim
Tel 89 82 51 15

P. ADAM
(wine)
Lauw
Tel 89 82 40 37

ALAIN STURM
(*boucher-charcutier*, delicatessen)
5 rue Vieil-Armand,
Cernay
Tel 89 75 42 65

CHRISTMANN
(*pâtisserie, salon de thé*)
8 place de l'Hôtel de Ville,
Guebwiller
Tel 89 74 27 44

DISCHINGER
(Alsace specialities, cheese)
2 Grand'rue, Munster
Tel 89 77 36 92

DANIEL JACQUAT
(butcher)
44 Grand'rue, Munster
Tel 89 77 19 36

GERARD WENDLING
(game, meat)
58 Grand'rue, Munster
Tel 89 77 36 64

JEAN-PAUL GILG
(*pâtisserie*, chocolates, ice cream)
11 Grand'rue, Munster
Tel 89 77 37 56

DOMAINE WEINBACH (CLOS DES
CAPUCINS)
(wine)
25 route du Vin, Kaysersberg
Tel 89 47 13 21

PATISSERIE LOECKEN
(*pâtisserie, Kougelhopf*)
46 rue Gral. de Gaulle,
Kaysersberg
Tel 89 47 34 35

JEAN-LOUIS BRUXER
(meat)
107 rue Gral. de Gaulle,
Kaysersberg
Tel 89 78 23 19

LE CELLIER DES MONTAGNES
(local specialities)
Hachimette
Tel 89 47 23 60

JACQUES HAXAIRE
(Munster)
Lapoutroie
Tel 89 47 50 76

CHRISTINE ET PATRICK CHAIZE
(Munster, mountain cheese)
215 Basses Huttes, Orbey
Tel 89 71 30 42

FERME DES PRES DU BOIS
(Munster, mountain cheese, dairy
products)
Orbey
Tel 89 71 22 11

LES CONFITURES DU CLIMONT
(jams)
La Salcée
Tel 88 97 72 01

F. MEYER
(*eaux-de-vie*)
19–20 rue Principale, Hohwarth
Tel 88 85 63 95

MARIE-FRANCOISE HUBRECHT
(*eaux-de-vie*)
8 rue de Kuhnenbach,
Maisonsgoutte
Tel 88 57 17 79

**Markets**

Monday: *Kaysersberg*
Tuesday: *Munster*
Wednesday: *Villé, Soultz, Orbey,
Masevaux*
Friday: *Lapoutroie*
Saturday: *Munster, Orbey, Thann*

**Fairs and festivals**

Ascension weekend: *Festival de Jazz*
(jazz festival), Munster
three Sundays before Easter: *Jeux de
la Passion* (Passion Play, in German),

Masevaux
April and October: *Fête du Tissu* (tex-
tile fair and market), Ste Marie-aux-
Mines
mid-May: *Foire aux Vins* (Wine festi-
val), Guebwiller
end of June: *Fête de la Cerise et du
Kirsch* (cherry and Kirsch festival),
Breitenbach
first weekend in July: *Bourse des
Minéraux* (precious stones market),
Sainte Marie-aux-Mines

second and third weekend in July:
*Rêve d'une Nuit d'Eté* (Midsummer
Night's Dream Son et Lumiére), Saint-
Pierre-Bois
last weekend in September: *Fête de la
Tourte* (tourte festival), Munster

*BELOW Lonely Vosges farmhouses
joined by steeply winding roads dot
the landscape in this little valley
above Lapoutroie.*
*OPPOSITE The river at Kaysersberg.*

# LIST OF RECIPES

# INDEX

**PUBLISHER'S ACKNOWLEDGMENTS**
Index    **Karin Woodruff**
Map      **Claire Melinsky**

For the recipe photography ( pages 32, 33, 34, 35, 37, 38, 40-1, 42, 45, 63, 65, 66, 68-9, 71, 72, 74, 91, 93, 95, 96, 97, 98, 101, 103, 118, 119, 120, 123, 125, 127, 128)
Home Economist    **Jane Suthering**
Assistant    **Katy Holder**
Stylist/Art Director    **Karen Bowen**

**AUTHOR'S ACKNOWLEDGMENTS**

Grateful thanks go to the chefs, butchers, bakers, winemakers, sommeliers, cheese-mongers, farmers and fishermen of Alsace, for their friendliness and generosity; the Comte de Poutales, Dédé Richert and Susy and René Stengel, our hunting hosts in northern Alsace; Soeur Esther of Erckartswiller, for her beautiful Springerle; Christiane Bisch, for many recipes and introductions; Jim Delaney, for introducing me to Winword; and Erica Rokweiler, for permitting another raid on her library and for reading the manuscript. My wonderful family were great fellow travellers, on the road and at the table, testing recipes. Thanks finally to Charlotte Coleman-Smith, Alison Bolus and Karen Bowen of Conran Octopus; to my agent Barbara Levy (a true friend of Alsace); and to Marianne Majerus for her magnificent photographs.

**PHOTOGRAPHER'S ACKNOWLEDGMENTS**

Photography in Alsace was a uniquely heartwarming experience. I was given a warm and generous welcome by many chefs, vintners and food producers whom I visited. Unfortunately they are too numer-ous to mention individually here, but I have not forgotten their kindness. My spe-cial thanks to Jean Michel and Gillian Edel who did their utmost to assist us during our stay at the Bouxhof. Thank you also to Karen and Ron Bowen, Jane Suthering and Katy Holder for their hard work and good humour; to Sue and Monty Style for their support and hospitality. Finally I would like to thank my family in London and Luxembourg: Robert and Nicolas Clark-Majerus and Blanche and Nicolas Majerus-Baron whose unstinting support was essential to the completion of this book.

## first course

Wild mushrooms 35                    68
Herring - apple - sour cream          68
mushroom - tomato quiche              68
onion tart - 69
v chicken - pork wine Terrine 70
chicken / sweetbreads in
            vol a vent - 99

### soup

lentil stew. 36
wild garlic 94

## VEGETABLES

v Potato-celeriac Gratin 70
grated potato pancakes
        with goats cheese - 39
baked leeks + potatoes - 39
carrot + celeriac 40
corn pancakes 95
cabbage, onion, chestnut 122

### salad

lettuce, mushroom foie gras 66
cheese on lettuce - 94
v stuffed crepes on greens 94
v potato with hardons +
        mustard dressing 121

## Poultry

Rabbit horseradish sauce 35
chicken - juniper berries - beer 43
v chicken wine + mushrooms 73
Rabbit stew 125

### Sea food

Sauerkraut - Salmon - Pastry 42

### Pork, Beef, Veal

Pork roast in pastry 64
v Ham + asparagus mousse 90
Haricot beans + sausage 100
v Lamb, beef + pork + veg - 100
cheese, bacon, potato pie 119

## Starches

spatzle 41
noodles 73

### Dessert

Hazelnut cake torte
    with fruit-meringue 44
kougel hopf 64
grape - walnut tart - 74
Alsace cheesecake 103
Pear + ginger pudding 119